YOU ARE NOT YOUR RACE

You Are Not Your Race

Embracing Our Shared
Humanity in a Chaotic Age

Fe Bencosme

LIONCREST
PUBLISHING

YOU ARE NOT YOUR RACE
Embracing Our Shared Humanity in a Chaotic Age

FIRST EDITION

ISBN   978-1-5445-3446-6 *Hardcover*
         978-1-5445-3445-9 *Paperback*
         978-1-5445-3447-3 *Ebook*

FOR MOMMIE Y PAPÁ

Contents

Introduction

"What are you?"

For people of mixed heritage in race-obsessed America, this is the question that hovers at the edge of our identity. Many of the loudest voices in our culture take it as an article of faith that everyone must classify themselves according to ready-made racial categories. While ultimately these classifications mean very little to me and many other Americans, we are all being forced to confront the increasingly strident voices of racial ideologues.

As someone born to a woman of African descent from the Virgin Islands and a father of European descent from the Dominican Republic, people cannot easily and immediately place me as "black" or "Latina," or any other ethnic or racial category for that matter. On rare occasions, a person will come right out and ask, "What are you?"

This would be viewed by many as an annoying and discourteous question, best responded to with a sigh and an eye roll, or perhaps even rage. But for me it is an ideal opportunity to challenge assumptions, and so I answer with questions of my own:

"What do you mean? Do you mean my ethnicity? My political identity? My race?"

I am always amused by the quizzical look I get back. Many of my fellow Americans are so locked into identifying people by the misconceived notion of racial category that they have trouble understanding someone who does not view the world through that lens.

My unwillingness to bind myself to a specific category is no longer safe and neutral ground in our culture. Why do I refuse to identify by race?

Before intelligent discussion can begin, it is important to get clear on terms. Many people—including those who ask the question "what are you?"—often mix together terms like race, ethnicity, and nationality.

Race is essentially an unreal category, culturally constructed and causing havoc in our culture. Ethnicity is the aggregate of our heritage and backgrounds. It is the language, cuisine, values, and traditions that get passed down through generations. Ethnicity is often confused with race, but ethnicity is the culture or cultures you identify with, such as Italian, Puerto Rican, German, etc.

Nationality is your legal political identity. If you are a legal American citizen, then your nationality is American. If a person legally switches citizenship, they have also changed nationalities.

Some cultures view ethnicity and nationality as inseparable. Dominicans are an example of this. United by a common history, language, and traditions, their pride in country is profound. And this despite a continuum of skin tones ranging from "white" on one end to "black" on the other, and every shade in between. Identifying with your ethnicity or nationality does not require a reference to "race" at all.

GETTING PERSPECTIVE

The fundamental premise of this book is that we are inflicting serious damage to ourselves as individuals and as a country because of our relentless focus on race. From my perspective, a person who grounds their identity in their outward characteristics and ancestry is a person who is severely limiting their freedom, both personally and politically.

While I would agree that people of mixed heritage are often given scant attention in our debates over racial ideology, I do not believe the lesson should be that we need to begin emphasizing biracial or multiracial as a category. I do not believe identifying as biracial, multiracial, or mixed heritage puts a person at a disadvantage in America. Nor do I believe doing so elevates a person to "victim" status in need of special protection.

In fact, the solution is quite the opposite.

WHAT IS RACE, REALLY?

Our national obsession with race is especially damaging when you consider that, strictly speaking, race does not exist. It is a socially and intellectually constructed category that gets very fuzzy when you hold it up to inspection. You may find it hard to get your head around the idea that race is a myth, but we will cover this concept in more detail in Chapter 2.

Race is an arbitrary category society has created, and so too are the terms biracial and multiracial. But since large swaths of our culture have accepted these racial categories as fundamentally true, concepts such as "black," "white," and "brown" have huge real-world impacts. Therefore, one of the things I hope to do in this book is to turn some of the accepted language of "race" on itself and show how hollow much of our race talk is. I will show how the very idea begins to crumble when you look closely at its contradictions.

This is not to say that I want to take away the freedom of anyone else to identify as black or white or brown or any other color or race. If I do not want to be judged for refusing to choose a category, it would be hypocritical to infringe on the different choices of others.

I even have some sympathy for the arguments and feelings of those who choose to identify by race and color. There are good historical reasons why it is paramount for many Americans of African descent to be seen as black, and unapologetically so. Many would say that it is important to be out front boldly when, for a significant part of American history, attempts were made to keep them out of sight.

However, understanding this position is not the same as agreeing. The weaponization of fallacy in the reckoning of historical grievances is counterproductive. This book will interrogate our obsession with race and color and ask how much more we might achieve as individuals and as a country if we took race off the table. What if we dropped all the qualifiers we use in front of "American" and identified simply as Americans, first and foremost?

While I do advocate detaching our identity from hard and fast racial categories, we do need a common language in order to communicate with each other. For expediency, I will use the current terms biracial, multiracial, mixed heritage, and multi-ethnic interchangeably. Also, it has become more common in the media to capitalize the word "black" when using it in a racial context. This is yet another symptom of our current cultural mania for emphasizing race and elevating it as an overwhelmingly dominant category. In keeping with this book's focus, the word black will remain lowercase. I will also occasionally use these terms with quotation marks to draw attention to the tenuous nature of these labels.

Continuing to use the language of labeling by race is problematic for me. With language, we can either diminish or emphasize a topic, and so for me to continue to make racial distinctions by language is somewhat painful. Black, brown, Hispanic, white, etc., all serve to divide us, and the more we use these words, the more we normalize dividing ourselves.

Our long-range goal should be to rid our language and talk of race-based descriptive qualifiers altogether. This will sometimes make our speech more inefficient and cumbersome, but we must try. However, to address the issues of race in this book, I must inevitably use some race-based words to explain what I am for and against.

A FRONT-ROW SEAT

You might be wondering who I am and why I have chosen to write this book. The genesis of my ideas about human identity were the cultures I experienced growing up. I spent my formative years in St. Croix, part of the Virgin Islands and a US territory. For years, everything I knew, touched, tasted, smelled was Crucian. I went to school with Crucian children and my gaggle of cousins were my playmates. I was lighter skinned than them, but it was not something that ever came up among us.

But I also spent a significant amount of my childhood in my father's hometown in the Dominican Republic. There too I lived, breathed, smelled, ate all things Dominican. My Dominican *primos* and the other children in the *campo* were my playmates. And my *abuelos* there loved me, too, although this time I was the one with darker skin. Again, nobody seemed to notice or care.

I cannot help but think that this childhood filled with two rich cultures gave me the gift of both knowing I was a part of them, but also an awareness that we cannot be reduced as humans to any one culture, race, or any other category.

Then I spent my high school years in New York with my mother and my two siblings, attending one of NYC's "specialized" high schools in Chelsea that was known for combining rigorous curriculum and the fine arts. Commuting into the city for school every day (two hours each way) awakened in me a taste for adventure and probably influenced my fascination with travel. It was in high school that others began to press their ideas about race on me, the beginning of a journey that led to this book.

As I have experienced life from the socially imposed category of "mixed race," I have had a front-row seat to many of the contradictions of how we talk about race in this country.

America is at a crossroads, and a dangerous one. We are pulling apart, trying to move in opposite directions, and bad ideology is beginning to move us down a dead-end road. Our politics are more divided than ever, and the evidence of the splits continually reveals itself in education, in political protests, and in how we talk about history:

- Children as young as five are taught to classify and divide themselves by race and skin color at school, with the claim that this is necessary for antiracist training.[1]
- "Multiracial" students are forced to sit through course lectures that demand they dissect the parts of themselves that are privileged.[2]
- The COVID-19 pandemic has seen patient protocols that call for using race to determine treatment priority, even when it overrides much higher risk factors.[3]

These are just a small handful of examples; the list of the ways race is being used for distorted purposes could be at least as long as this book. We are pushing our children to see every-

---

1   Bion Bartning, "Dividing by Race Comes to Grade School," opinion, Wall Street Journal, March 7, 2021, https://www.wsj.com/articles/dividing-by-race-comes-to-grade-school-11615144898.

2   Colin Wright (@SwipeWright), " BREAKING: Lawsuit filed today against educational agencies, teachers, principal, & CEO responsible for hosting workshops requiring children to make public professions about their racial, sexual, gender & religious identities, some of which were singled out for interrogation," Twitter, December 23, 2020, 1:23 a.m., https://threadreaderapp.com/thread/1341645599578308609.html.

3   Centers for Disease Control and Prevention, "Health Equity Considerations & Racial & Ethnic Minority Groups," updated January 25, 2022, https://www.cdc.gov/coronavirus/2019-ncov/community/health-equity/race-ethnicity.html.

thing through the lens of racial ideology, and consequently de-emphasizing our common humanity. What many of these activists do not seem to realize is that they are building toward a world the exact opposite of what they claim to want. The more we obsess about race, the more we validate the false and dehumanizing idea that people can be reduced to made-up categories with no grounding in truth.

I am writing this book because it is needed. Race is being propagandized to divide us. And it appears the race hustlers are succeeding to the detriment of our Union. Every person needs to do something to preserve the country. This is my contribution.

I am also writing this because I think I can bring a needed but often neglected perspective.

Life has not always been pleasant for me as a person who embraces all parts of my identity. As a teen, I was often ostracized for the mixed heritage I was born into—and sometimes brutally so. My adult life has seen much of the same. The details of the experiences change, but the reason for the marginalization remains.

Throughout this book I will share the hurtful, confusing, and sometimes debilitating experiences in my life as a person of mixed heritage in academia, in my romantic life, in my church, and in other areas of my life.

It is my hope this book will give voice to a perspective that is often completely ignored by the loudest and most ideological voices in race debates. The 2020 US census included 33 million people who classified themselves as multiracial, which is 10 percent of the total population. Yet most of the people shouting at each other about race on television and online opinion pieces rarely capture, or omit altogether, the truth about who we really are. It is hard to hold onto a simplistic viewpoint on race once you understand that we do not neatly fit into any single category, yet this is rarely talked about.

The other perspective I bring has grown out of my extensive life travels. I have had the good fortune to travel through nearly fifty countries across six continents, experiencing widely varying cultures, practices, and viewpoints. Yet I have noticed amazingly similar human aspirations that supersede the differences.

One of my most formative travel experiences was an eighteen-month solo sojourn throughout the Middle East soon after 9/11. I will share some stories from my travels that also helped to shape my view that racial categories are grossly misleading, and that common human values and motivations are much truer to life as it is lived.

I currently use my education in English and linguistics as a psychometrician, mostly testing foreign speakers of English for university placement and career placement in multinational corporations or nongovernmental agencies. I think it is worth noting that for many of those I test, a job or admission to a university in America, a country that is still viewed around the world as a place of tolerance and opportunity—not a place of hatred and repression as often portrayed in our own media—is a dream come true.

FREE YOURSELF

We have become a nation full of media and cultural commentary that encourages resentment and stokes anger. Although I do believe that more anger and resentment comes from racial ideologues than from those who oppose them, it must be said that people on all sides get caught up in proving the other side wrong, rather than in productive solutions. Sadly, too, I have at times allowed myself to fall victim to this mindset.

I spend a good portion of this book dismantling the false ideas surrounding race that have taken root in our culture. I do this because I want readers to have better, more reasoned arguments to defeat racial ideologues in the marketplace of ideas. But I have no interest in giving readers the tools to sharpen their rhetorical knives. That would be counterproductive.

We need to accept that no one book, editorial, or blog post is going to solve our ideological divisions. There is no magic pill that creates sudden agreement and harmony. However, what we can do as individuals is free ourselves from misguided obsessions and categories, and live our lives as human beings, not identity groups.

To that end, this book culminates in a list of guidelines for a better path forward. By de-centering race, you will not only free yourself, you will also become a contributor to a less polarized and healthier nation.

Ultimately, that is what this book is about: how to be free from ideologies that are pushing you to see yourself as a category or reduce you to a group of arbitrary racial characteristics. This reduction of people to racial categories is the lie that seems to be taking a deeper hold in American life. It is time to end that lie and realize that everyone's skin has a color, and it is just one small part of who we are.

You can resist those who insist that your political goals, your life aspirations, and your very identity are determined by race. And this can be done without anger or resentment. As you will see in the chapters that follow, you are not your race. Understanding this is very freeing.

CHAPTER 1

Journeying Through the World of Humans

"For small creatures such as we the vastness is bearable only through love."

—CARL SAGAN, AMERICAN ASTRONOMER

On December 11, 2001, three months to the day after 9/11, I was on a plane headed to the Middle East. I had already delayed the trip once, unsure if I should be traveling to the geographic heart of Islamic culture with tensions so high.

Whatever hesitancy I felt, there I was, airplane seatbelt on, about to fly to Cairo, which would be my home base for the next eighteen months. I would also take eye-opening (and sometimes hair-raising!) forays into Syria, Jordan, and Iraq. What I learned on those adventures would be formative for my thinking about race, nationality, and avoiding stereotypes.

I start with these stories to emphasize that our common

humanity across cultures, colors, and nations is not some vague, feel-good claptrap, but a fundamental fact of reality. If we can see and remember that, we can apply it to our own culture that is so divided along race and ideology today.

What made me decide to get on a plane to the Middle East? There is no one simple answer to that, but 9/11 was definitely the catalyst in more ways than one.

As part of my work as a media relations director for a hotel company, I was supposed to have been in Bermuda on 9/11. But as it happened, my boss and I had switched up the plan at the last minute; she went to the conference in Bermuda, and I stayed behind at our office in Miami.

Back in 2001, everyone in the world was not yet glued to their smartphones, and social media was not yet omnipresent. I was never one for watching television (I didn't even own one until 2008) so, for most of the morning, I was completely oblivious to the news coming out of New York. It was a shock when my boss called me from Bermuda sounding very anxious and told me about the planes hitting the towers.

My next phone call was to my longtime friend and eventual husband. He was at his desk in Washington, DC near the Pentagon when the third plane hit. The last words I heard from him were "Oh, sh–! They hit the Pentagon!" The phone went dead. It would be a full day before I heard from him again.

I went through all the emotions that Americans felt over the next days and weeks as we mourned what felt unthinkable. As some of the shock wore off, I began to grapple with the economic impact in my own industry. Travel plummeted and layoffs were sure to follow.

One morning in October 2001 I was so depressed by my role as a publicist in the midst of a national crisis, I could barely bring myself to go in. I stayed in bed and sobbed. About mid-morning, my phone started ringing off the hook. I assumed it was my boss looking for me, and I was right. But she was not wondering where I was, she wanted to tell me that I was about to be laid off and wanted to cushion the blow.

For me, that layoff would be a blessing. It made a decision for me that I had not been able to make for myself. I had grown disenchanted with my work in media relations. Dealing with the media is very transactional; journalists have biases and are skilled at manipulation. To be fair, I was also working to get my company portrayed in the best light. Everyone was out for themselves and the whole thing just felt fake to me.

I was given the option to stop working right away and I took it. After some soul searching and some tough love advice from an older, wiser friend, I made the decision to return to the Middle East. I had been there on a ten-day business trip only two months before and wanted to visit again with more time to explore.

Of course, if all I had wanted was to travel, I could have picked another part of the world that was not so fraught with tension. I thought momentarily about going to the Dominican Republic to spend some extended time with family. But 9/11 had not only pushed me out of my job; it also had me questioning what I was reading in the news.

The portrayals of Islamic peoples and cultures seemed designed to keep us on a war footing. What happened on 9/11 was of course very real, so it was undeniable that some bad actors hated America. But I wondered how deep that went and what most of the people were like. Were we being fed stereotypes and exaggerations about people? I wanted to know firsthand.

So, throwing my fate to the winds, I decided to go. That older, wiser friend who gave me that tough love advice also connected me with someone who could help me secure an apartment in Cairo.

Living in a radically different part of the world for an extended period impacts you in so many ways. One of the biggest lessons for me, and one directly relevant for this book, was that you cannot reduce the complexity and beauty of people to their race or nationality.

The only generalization I found you could make is that in every culture and race, you will find mostly good people who want the same things: a chance to make a decent living and to protect their children and give them a future. Given the chance, many will help others, even strangers, in very concrete ways.

Three snapshots from my time traveling in the Middle East will illustrate what I mean.

SNAPSHOT 1: SYRIA

In late March 2003, I decided to visit Syria. I was on a tight budget, so I took the trip by bus, arriving at the depot around 2 a.m. I found a cab to take me to the hostel where I would stay during my visit.

Despite the late hour, I talked virtually nonstop to the taxi driver, perhaps because I was wired with the excitement and nervousness of visiting a new country. Between running my mouth and being amped up, I was apparently too distracted. I failed to notice that I never returned my wallet to its place in my backpack.

I reached the front door of the hostel and came up empty when I fished around in my pack for my wallet and passport. I turned back toward the cab in a futile attempt to flag the driver, but he had already pulled away.

I now had no money. Even worse, I had no identification or passport. I am not generally the panicking type, but I was immediately worried. When traveling in a country with a repressive, authoritarian government, your American passport feels like a security blanket. Mine had just driven away in that cab.

Whatever the larger problems I had just created for myself, I had a more immediate one in front of me. I did not even have identification to show the clerk at the hostel. Standing behind the front desk was a tall Syrian man who looked as if he could have easily been from India or Malaysia. This is something I would notice again and again in my travels; on an individual level, many people do not conform to our preconceived ideas of how someone of a particular nationality will look.

Whatever his heritage, this kind man would become my interpreter and my guide as I made my way through a maze of bureaucracy for the next ten days. But at two in the morning, he was no doubt tired, and likely wanted nothing more than to get this suddenly anxious young American woman away from him before she broke down in tears.

He told me not to worry about the problem tonight, to go up to my room, and that we would figure something out in the morning. It calmed me to know I at least had a place to sleep that night, and his gentle manner was reassuring. As things would turn out, the man in front of me would be my best ally in navigating Syrian culture and politics on my journey to find a way out of the country.

The next morning, I began trying to dig myself out of the hole. First, I reached out to have money wired to me. Then, that kind clerk accompanied me to the cab company to help translate. If the taxi driver found my wallet, he apparently did not turn it in.

The hostel clerk explained that he was not surprised. Why take the risk of turning in a foreigner's passport and possibly have questions raised about how it came into his possession? The level of repression and fear that people could feel under these kinds of regimes began to sink in. The safer, smarter choice is to never do anything to draw unwanted attention to yourself.

It also made me suddenly realize that this kindly clerk was putting himself at risk by helping me. This became even more clear when he would eventually accompany me to a Syrian police headquarters. I had been reissued a passport, but I needed a certain signature to get the stamps I needed to get out of the country, and this would be the toughest signature to get.

Of course, I did not know the ins and outs of Syrian police structure in the early 2000s, but I was told that where I needed to go was a location of the "secret" police. If that meant they operated outside normal legal constraints, I had no problem believing it.

The whole building was fenced and required visitors to be escorted through a huge rusty gate. It was almost as if we were in a movie. The hostel clerk chaperoned me to that point, but he was not permitted to enter.

I walked in and saw extreme degradation, including male and female prisoners chained to walls and beds in the same room. I soon found myself in front of a large, intimidating man, tawny-skinned with jet black hair and a thick mustache. He screamed at me in Arabic for what seemed an eternity, seemingly testing me to see if I understood the language. When he was satisfied that I could not, he began speaking in English. He was still gruff, but he calmed down and I got the signature I needed.

The decency and courage of this ordinary hostel clerk is something that has stayed with me through the decades since. It has embedded itself in my experience of life as a reminder that we are not our nationality or our race. Those things influence us, but they are never who we are.

One other lasting image has stayed with me all through the years since. I had at last gotten everything I needed to get out of Syria, and I was at the final border crossing. This ill-fated venture was finally over and I could see Jordan on the other side right in front of me. I faced the border guard, who with his very light skin tone was yet another example of a Syrian who did not conform to how we "expect" Syrians to look. He checked my passport and slowly raised his stamp and brought it down. He began to hand the passport back to me, but then pulled it back.

Then he said in English, "Go home and tell your countrymen

we do not have a problem with them." He handed me back my passport and I was finally free to go.

SNAPSHOT 2: UNEXPECTED HOSPITALITY IN JORDAN

Another trip I took during my time in the Middle East was on a cargo ship from Nuweiba, Egypt, to the city of Aqaba, the nearest port in Jordan.

A speed boat would have been faster, but instead, my tight budget and I were on this boat with poor Egyptians and cattle. It felt like a grand adventure but quickly became less fun when I noticed a man shadowing me wherever I went on the ship.

As a twenty-something woman traveling alone, I could be a target for unsavory characters. It is also worth noting that a woman traveling alone in a Muslim country stands out more than in the United States.

My initial strategy was to just keep moving until I lost the guy, but that was not working. Finally, I heard two male voices speaking English, and I decided to slide in next to them and join in the conversation.

It turned out one was an American of Pakistani descent who had been studying in Damascus, Syria, and the other a young Palestinian man living in Jordan with his father. I was also relieved to discover that my ploy seemed to have worked: my follower wandered away when he saw me interacting with others.

We reached Aqaba, and we and several others boarded a big taxi bus and were off to Amman, the capital, several hours' drive away. The Palestinian's father was there to greet him when we left the bus. He offered to drop me off at my hostel and I accepted. We arrived and the father took one look at it and said I could not stay in such a place. Instead, he insisted I come stay with their family and experience true hospitality.

You may be familiar with the tradition still practiced in many Arab cultures of offering strangers and wayfarers three days of hospitality. This idea has deep roots, going back to ancient biblical times.

Still, as a young woman traveling alone, I probably should have been wary of hopping in a car with strangers. However, every signal was telling me the offer was genuine, so off I went.

It turned out to be a wonderful and memorable three days spent with this beautiful family. There was the father, the son, and his twin sister. Another son lived there with his wife. What sticks out in my mind is how delightful each meal was, with all of us sitting on the floor and enjoying each other's company. This was true fellowship offered to an American woman when they had nothing to gain from it.

SNAPSHOT 3: IRAQ ON THE BRINK OF OPERATION SHOCK AND AWE

In my wide-eyed passion to find out more about what was going on in the Middle East, I found a way into Iraq in early 2003, just weeks before the United States was to begin Operation Shock and Awe, the start of the Iraq War.

I had managed to finagle a press pass as a stringer from a tiny newspaper under the assumption that I would report a story of a group of "human shield" protestors who were gathering in and around Iraq. They planned on strategically placing their bodies where the bombs were to fall in hopes this would sway the US government to not commence bombing.

I still have that press pass, but alas, I never filed a story. It might have made a good story, too, because by happenstance, I ended up rooming with Faith Fippinger[4] for a brief time in Jordan as we prepared to enter Iraq. Faith, a retired American school teacher, became the best known of the human shields and was later prosecuted by the US government for her actions.

There are three moments in Iraq I will never forget, each of them once again reminding me of the beauty of humans and the irrelevance of their race or nationality.

The first was wedding day in Iraq. Thursday is the traditional day for weddings in Arab cultures, at least among the common people. On this particular Thursday, with the bombing looming in the near future, people were still getting married and expressing joy.

For these street weddings, there are no private invitations. The husband and wife take a public stroll with family in tow, and whoever shows up is welcome to join in with the dancing and celebrating. It was a mash-up of skin and eye colors and hair textures, a touching scene made more so by the context of imminent war.

---

4   Jennifer Frey, "'Human Shields,' Armed with Prayers," The Washington Post, March 18, 2003, https://www.washingtonpost.com/archive/lifestyle/2003/03/18/human-shields-armed-with-prayers/dad65007-506a-41b7-82c1-56c794f56450.

The second moment was extremely fleeting but moving. A little Iraqi boy came out of nowhere on the street and handed me a flower. There was something in this freckle-faced, red-headed little boy that connected us strongly for just that moment of exchange. It is a flower I keep pressed in a frame with Psalm 139, which I was carrying in my breast pocket at the time.

The third moment came when I was on a tour of Iraq with a caravan of volunteer human shields. The Iraqi government was a willing partner in taking the human shields through the country. One of the stops was historic Babylon.

Without a doubt, the tour involved meeting people approved by government officials to say what was in their interests. But at that stop in Babylon, I spoke with a woman who spoke so sincerely that it left me with no doubt that she was speaking from the heart.

I asked her how she felt about the bombing that would almost certainly begin soon. She was sure she and her family would survive it, but it was what would come after that scared her.

Would her sons begin to lose their values if the United States took over Iraq? She did not know. She told me they had a custom of meeting for daily lunch, something she feared would go by the wayside in favor of fast food. She agonized over whether they would become more materialistic and be exposed to hyper-sexualized images on television.

Whether her specific fears and feelings were right or wrong is not for me to judge. What impacted me the most was hearing a mother talk about trying to keep her family together. It made me realize that what motivates almost everyone—white, black, multiracial, "Arab," American, whatever—is the same for people everywhere. We all want to be able to carve out a meaningful and sustainable living; keep our families together; preserve the things that bind us; and survive tough times like war.

You cannot listen to a mother under the threat of war and radical societal change express concern for her children and not understand that we live in a world of individual humans with all their hope, love, and fear.

DIVIDING PEOPLE

Do we not all have stories in our memory bank that remind us that skin color, phenotypes, and nationality cannot predict individual human behavior? Yours may be more dramatic or less so, but they are there.

Why then is so much talk in America today about simplistic divisions of people into oppressors and victims? Why are some people demonized and others elevated based on nothing more than outward characteristics?

It is because we have allowed the lie of race to override the true, complex stories we all have about interacting with people of all colors. The conversation in America has come to be dominated by voices that insist race determines much of our individual behavior and our ability to connect with one another. Yet, all over the planet at every moment, humans are proving that race does not have to matter, unless we let it.

Much of the rest of the book will be devoted to taking on race as it plays out in science, education, politics, and more. My hope is that as you read through it, you will carry the spirit of this first chapter with you. You are journeying through a world full of humans, not a world of racial tribes.

CHAPTER 2

Is Race Even Real?

"Facts are stubborn things, but, as someone wisely said, not half as stubborn as fallacies."

—LUCY MAUD MONTGOMERY, CANADIAN AUTHOR

Among the deluge of information available on the US government's census website is this startling fact:

"The Multiracial population has changed considerably since 2010. It was measured at 9 million people in 2010 and is now 33.8 million people in 2020, a 276% increase."[5]

In just ten years' time, the number of people identifying as multiracial increased by more than 24 million. The total has now reached 10 percent of the total US population.

---

5 Nicholas Jones et al., "Improved Race and Ethnicity Measures Reveal U.S. Population Is Much More Multiracial," United States Census Bureau, August 12, 2021, https://www. census.gov/library/stories/2021/08/improved-race-ethnicity-measures-reveal-united-states-population-much-more-multiracial.html.

One insight to draw from this is that the simple black/brown/ white categories dominating much race talk in the media fails to grapple with the complexity of actual humans. If at least one out of every ten Americans does not fit neatly into these created categories, how useful are they really? As a person of mixed heritage, I know simplistic groupings are virtually worthless for understanding the lives of specific individuals.

But there is something else buried in this statistic that is interesting: the basis for determining race in this country depends upon how people *self-identify*. In other words, it is about the box or boxes people choose for themselves on the census form.

The whole concept of encouraging people to check boxes is problematic for reasons that should be obvious. I am tempted to say none of this box-checking matters because it does not change who you are as an individual. That is true, but there is still harm. The statistics generated by the census are subsequently used by academics, activists, pollsters, and politicians to dream up new social engineering schemes grounded in reductive racial categories. We would be better off without them.

There is another crucial point to grasp here, too. There is a large element of arbitrary choice in all this. We tend to read these race statistics from the census results as if they were a completely objective and totally accurate reflection of reality. It becomes ingrained in all of us that we must fit into some category. The truth is a lot more complicated, and it would be better for all of us to acknowledge that race is in large part an arbitrary construction we individually choose (or reject).

Yet our political, educational, and cultural bureaucracies have put so much emphasis on categories that have no meaningful, intrinsic standards. Even worse, more and more people are allowing a distorted focus on race to tell them that their racial status is fundamental to the success or failure of their lives.

There is something else interesting here. No doubt part of that 276 percent increase is attributable to greater cultural acceptance of what we have chosen to call "intermarriage" and "interracial relationships." But this large of an increase strongly suggests that more people are choosing "multiracial" when they did not make that same choice on the last census. Are there really that many cross-cultural marriages taking place, or is there more pressure not to identify as "white" than there was ten years ago? Does it now feel more mandatory to take a stand on your racial status against "whiteness" if at all possible?

I believe the answers to these questions are *yes* and *yes*. At least some of this huge increase is grounded in people's evolving perception of identity, and their choices are strongly influenced by the flood of cultural messages about race that have become so prominent.

The self-declaration aspect of racial identity gives a clue that race may be a somewhat arbitrary category. The interesting thing is that science agrees. The growing evidence of genetic variation in what we historically call "race" indicates that there are no unifying genetic characteristics among people considered to be of a specific race.

At its root, race is a social construct. However, race in many cases has become the basis for a religious-like ideology and the absolute foundation of personal identity. When a construct is used in this way, it turns poisonous, both for the individual and for society.

One example of this is Directive No. 15,[6] or Race and Ethnic Standards for Federal Statistics and Administrative Reporting. Established during the Carter Administration by the Office of Management and Budget (OMB) as guidelines for collecting and presenting data on race and ethnicity, the memo explicitly states that the racial categories "should not be interpreted as being scientific or anthropological in nature" (or "viewed as determinants of eligibility for participation in any Federal Program" for that matter). In 1997 when the directive underwent a review process, the then Committee for the Review of the Racial and Ethnic Standards to OMB further clarified that Directive No. 15 "does not tell an individual who he or she is, or specify how an individual should classify himself or herself."[7] We now know nothing could be further from the truth given the prevalence of critical race theory in our institutions.

When I say that race is a human construct, am I saying it is not real? Yes, I really am saying that race is not a fundamental reality.

Guy P. Harrison, in his book *Race and Reality: What Everyone Should Know About Our Biological Diversity*, provides an illuminating illustration of cultural constructions and how we can mistake them for reality. To demonstrate, he asks the reader how many oceans are there. Most people will answer five, which

---

6   Race and Ethnic Standards for Federal Statistics and Administrative Reporting, Office of Management and Budget Directive No. 15, (May 12, 1977), reviewed Nov. 19, 2019, https://wonder.cdc.gov/wonder/help/populations/bridged-race/directive15.html.

7   Review of the Racial and Ethnic Standards to the OMB Concerning Changes..., Office of Management and Budget, (July 9, 1997): Part II, pp. 36,873–946, https://obamawhitehouse.archives.gov/omb/fedreg_directive_15/.

is correct, but only because that is how we have chosen to represent the oceans on a map.

However, as Harrison points out, if you use your finger to trace the flow of the oceans around the globe, you will see that it is one continuous body of water. In reality, there is only one ocean in the world. Studying the ocean is sometimes easier with points of reference, so we have named five oceans. This is useful, but at the same time it is also misleading and technically incorrect.

This analogy is even more compelling when you consider that until recently, the right answer would have been four oceans. The consensus now is to call the Southern Ocean off the coast of Antarctica an ocean. Before that was added, there were said to be only four oceans: the Atlantic, Pacific, Indian, and Arctic.

The concept of race is analogous to the oceans example. Race is a simplistic and imprecise construct at the level of the individual. It *may* have some value for certain kinds of analysis, for example, focus groups or qualitative research with results applied narrowly, but that does not change the fact that race is constructed and not fundamentally real. If you trace your finger over the flow of humanity, there is no place where you can say one race begins and another ends. This might sound outlandish to some readers, as if I were saying something akin to claiming that the Atlantic Ocean is not real. However, in a basic sense, both the Atlantic Ocean and races are not real.

A person of mixed heritage can perhaps more easily and intuitively grasp that race is constructed and is slippery ground for building an identity. You know you do not fit neatly into any one racial category. Once you start looking more closely at how these categories are constructed, you begin to see the cracks in the façade and begin to question the whole edifice of racial ideology.

Of course, I'm not making a blanket statement here that all multiethnic people hold my view. Some strongly identify with a particular cultural category. And of course, you do not have to identify as multiethnic to understand that race is constructed. It is simply to state that people with mixed backgrounds are often confronted in a more concrete way with the contradictions of the reigning racial orthodoxies.

THE ARCHITECTS OF "RACE"

We tend to think of race as a hard and fast biological reality. It is not. It is a constructed category with a history of masquerading as science. Here is a very concise guide to some of the people who created the problematic category we are still dealing with today:

1. Associating people with skin color started with Carolus Linnaeus, Swedish botanist (1707–1778), known as the father of taxonomy. He classified humans under the order of Primates and divided them further by geography and skin color—e.g., whitish Europeans, reddish Americans, tawny Asians, blackish Africans.

2. Linnaeus divvied people up by skin color, but Johann Friedrich Blumenbach, German anthropologist (1752–1840), took it a step further. His barometer was cranial size (differences he attributed to geography, diet, and...skin color. Yikes—not exactly scientific!) Blumenbach's races are similar to Linnaeus', with Caucasian being

white and American, red. He replaces African with Ethiopian, Asian with Mongolian, and adds a Malay, or brown, category encompassing Pacific Islanders.

3. Then along comes Franz Boas, American anthropologist (born in Germany) 1858–1942, who tosses out race essentialism and instead examines human variation—physical and cultural—across and within populations. Some called it measuring how lived experience influences behavior. Boas vehemently opposed elevating any culture as superior to another.

4. Finally, Ashley Montagu, British-born American anthropologist (1905–1999) and author of the seminal text *Man's Most Dangerous Myth: The Fallacy of Race* (1942) was a student of Boas. Montagu correctly called out those who have misused the term race. "In biology, race is defined as a subdivision of species which inherits physical characteristics distinguishing it from other populations of the species. In this sense, there are many human 'races.' *But this is not the sense in which many anthropologists, race classifiers, and racists have used them*"[8] (emphasis added).

THE SILLINESS OF DNA 'PERCENTAGES'

The growing popularity of DNA testing services like Ancestry, 23andMe, and similar companies is also having an impact on people's perceptions of racial and ethnic categories. The way the results are sometimes framed encourages the illusion that race and ethnicity are stable categories through time.

It is not my intention to attack these companies. Many people

---

8   Ashley Montagu, *Man's Most Dangerous Myth: The Fallacy of Race* (New York: Columbia University Press, 1942).

use the results to help them build family trees, connect with relatives, and get a general sense of their national heritage. All that is to the good. In fact, I used these tests myself when I wanted to confirm my parents really were my parents and that I was not some child they were raising as their own, which is not uncommon in Virgin Islands culture or where adoption is out of the question, as in Dominican culture.

It also seems likely that as more data is collected, it will lead to deeper insights by scientists on human origins, DNA patterns, and who knows what other exciting discoveries.

But there is something science has already discovered about DNA and human history that is often ignored or outright rejected: racial characteristics are not stable over time; there are no immutable racial categories.

If you send in your saliva sample to one of these companies, what you will get back is an analysis of your "origins" by percentage. Imagine your DNA produces a 50 percent origin in West Africa, a 35 percent origin in Eastern Europe, and the other 15 percent is distributed among several other geographic locations.

Many people automatically translate this into racial terms. In this case, that 50 percent origin is often treated as a confirmation of a specific identity. It is further assumed that you are in some sense bonded with others who may have a similarly large percentage of West African DNA.

However, the science of DNA does not agree with that assumption. In terms of your overall genetic patterns, your specific

DNA markers are just as likely to have as much in common with any random person as with a person who shows a similar percentage of West African DNA origin.

How is that possible? One of the major factors is that the world of our ancestors going back a couple hundred thousand years has changed radically. Genetic traits are modified as climate conditions change, and as people migrate to different parts of the world, their genes manifest in new ways.

In addition, so much genetic mixing has occurred over human history that everyone's specific DNA can be said to have taken its own long, circuitous journey. That person you share some common DNA origins with has taken a completely different path. (A fun fact I learned from my own DNA test is that I share a common ancestor with Nelson Mandela!)

This is not intended as a deep analysis of the science of DNA. I am not a geneticist, and I am sure if we dug even more into the details, the picture would become even more nuanced. My point is to shake us out of lazy assumptions and complacency about what we all think we know about DNA, race, and common characteristics. These popular notions that DNA is something fixed through time that should therefore tell us something fundamental about ourselves does not hold up to scientific inspection.

Setting aside the scientific point of view for now and looking at percentages from a purely common sense perspective unravels the silliness further. How much sense would it make if someone were to say, for example, "I'm 50 percent black, I'm 30 percent Slavic, I'm 15 percent Spanish and 5 percent English"?

It is interesting to note that the world as we know it today does not reflect the world of two thousand years ago. Borders have shifted, and massive sections of land have been unified under single governments. Some have been torn apart while others simply ceased to exist. Take, for example, the area we now call England. As early as the fifth century, the land was inhabited by numerous ethnically Germanic tribes originating from areas currently known as France, Belgium, and The Netherlands.

The real question should be the impact and meaning for the individual person of being part of a Slavic, Spanish, or English culture. These are cultures, and they have no intrinsic biological meaning.

A good example of how silly it can get was revealed when Senator Elizabeth Warren released DNA results purportedly to establish her Native American heritage. What followed was a noisy debate about whether a small amount of her DNA meant she could legitimately identify as a member of the Cherokee Nation.

The science could not say how many generations this sliver of DNA went back, since test results become less and less clear the further you go back in time. But more directly to the point, the whole thing reveals how quickly arguing about who qualifies as what race becomes futile. Why do we use up so much energy worrying about who is supposedly what? Too often, the answer seems to be to gain preference in hiring, education, or political power.

I support Warren's freedom, like anyone's, to choose to identify with her heritage how she wishes. If she chose to highlight trace amounts of Native American ancestry for professional advancement in an academic environment focused on racial quotas, as some claim she did, then shame on her. But whatever her motivations, the more fundamental point is how many of our debates about race center around things that cannot be solved with any kind of certainty, do not help us lead more productive and happy lives, and ultimately do not speak to who we are as human beings.

The contradictions of racial categories pile one on top of another under close inspection. Yet we spend enormous quantities of energy twisting ourselves in knots about who belongs in what box and who has the "right" to choose that box. Our country and its citizens get lost in a maze of made-up identities and pointless debates about who qualifies as what.

For those who insist on identifying in these ways, we should at a minimum stop judging them and obsessing over whether they qualify as the ethnic or racial identity they claim. Of course, better still would be to stop worrying about choosing an identity grounded in race or ethnicity at all.

THE ONE-DROP RULE

Perhaps the height of absurdity is when a person or group attempts to dictate to another person that they must identify with a specific racial category.

One manifestation of the idea that you *must* identify a certain way is sometimes called the one-drop rule. Proponents of this rule say that if you have any heritage deemed to reach back into Africa (one drop of African blood), then you are black.

I find this idea wrong on its face, and also deeply irritating. As a woman with a dark-skinned mother, I have been told several times in my life that I am required to identify as black. A particularly memorable example happened on a dinner date. When asked about my identity, the man on the other side of the table interrupted my reply to say, "I don't care who you *think* you are, I am here to tell you..." I didn't hear the rest of what he said because I had stood up from the table and left the restaurant before he could finish.

Part of what I find so deeply irritating about all this is that identifying as black is apparently mandatory in the eyes of many, but no thought seems to be given to how this erases my Dominican heritage, or at least implies that my father is somehow persona non grata.

Am I being called on to cut my father out of the picture as though he never existed? I emphatically reject that I should in any way deny my father because of the color of his skin or his European heritage.

For the racial ideologues, nothing but total agreement with their view of the world is enough. They insist that my family history mandates acceptance of things that go to the core of who I am. That I must vote a certain way (for policies and politicians that claim to promote the best interests of the black community) and affirm approved beliefs (that I am oppressed by a white power structure).

Making this both deeply ironic and doubly frustrating is that it does not seem to dawn on these racial ideologues that they are using the exact same criteria and arguments that the most hard-core segregationists used in nineteenth and twentieth century America. They too were obsessed with the tiniest details of ancestry, blood, and color. In fact, the one-drop rule originated in post-slavery society and was codified in a 1924 Racial Integrity Act (and later overturned in 1967 with the US Supreme Court case *Loving v. Virginia*).

The segregationists used the one-drop rule as a weapon of exclusion and discrimination. The civil rights movement in the 1960s, the one that focused on the content of our character instead of the color of skin, fought that and won. Now the one-drop rule is back, but this time to coerce adherence to a political dogma, and with a frightening long-term goal for the world, it seems.

I acknowledge that there are still going to be people who cannot shake the idea that race is not an objective category. The concept is so ingrained in us because historically it has been created and used as a tool to hold power over others. Even today, there are fringe supremacy movements that claim to want to push us back to all that.

So, race is an abstraction, an invention, a creation of imagination, but it has undoubtedly had real-world impacts. The question becomes how can we free ourselves from this trap of racial categories? The way forward is to recognize how much pain these categories have caused. We are not going to free ourselves by continuing to pretend race is a stable, objective category that provides useful information about individuals. It does not; it just keeps us trapped in the same old tired labyrinth.

The way out of this maze is to firmly reject the notion that racial identification can tell us something fundamental about ourselves and others. As Bob Marley sang in his "Redemption Song," "Emancipate yourself from mental slavery. None but ourselves can free our minds." We have to do that at the level of the individual, which is the only level where we meaningfully interact.

Even if you are not ready to completely agree that race is a myth, I hope you are beginning to, at a minimum, question all the energy we pour into it. We need to start doing this fast, because our preoccupation with race is being turned into faulty lessons for our children.

CHAPTER 3

What Are We Teaching Our Children About Race?

"The wise man is a happy child."

—ARNAUD DESJARDINS, FRENCH AUTHOR,
DOCUMENTARIAN, AND MYSTIC

During my high school years, I lived in the Bayswater section of Far Rockaway, NY, with my mother and siblings. This neighborhood was situated on the farthest end of the Rockaway Peninsula, just before the county line with Long Island. When we moved in, it was a neighborhood just beginning a transition from predominantly Jewish to a diverse community of immigrants of different heritages.

By the time I was in my sophomore year, the transition was well underway, and the neighborhood was a true melting pot. I do not remember a lot of tensions, so it was a bit of a shock to be leaving for school one morning and finding "N-word get out" spray painted in big, bright blue letters on our street.

I was about fourteen when this happened, and although I was not completely unaware that race was an issue in America, intercommunity tension did not feel omnipresent. My recollection was that ethnicity was a more prominent part of people's identity at that time. We referred to and thought of people as belonging to the culture of their ancestral heritage or religion. There were the Irish kids, the Puerto Ricans, the Italians, the Jews, the Dominicans, and so on. Of course, there was the awareness of skin color, but connections to hues and tones and power were much less pronounced.

So seeing this racial epithet was confusing. I went back into the house and called my mother outside to see it. Her reaction, at least outwardly, was mild. It more or less boiled down to "Well, okay, you go have a good day at school."

That afternoon when I returned home, the word was gone, and that was the end of it. My mother felt no need to discuss it.

From the vantage point of decades later, this may seem to some a peculiar reaction at best, and a damaging, unhealthy one at worst. As a culture, we have become so convinced that children need to analyze their feelings about everything that happens and that all ignorant acts of hate must be confronted with maximum pushback, that we cannot see any other way.

But there are other ways. It is not my intent to say that true acts of discrimination should not be exposed and made right. I am also not saying that hateful rhetoric should not be called out and calmly opposed. However, we do need to think carefully about our responses and whether we do more self-damage when we give these kinds of incidents too much oxygen.

A story my mother told me revealed that she knew how to respond to disdain and derision in her own quiet way. Once while boarding a plane in Puerto Rico, she overheard two women fretting about having to sit next to her. The women were speaking in Spanish, apparently presuming my mother could not understand. What happened next told me what my mother was made of. She related to me in a tone of calm satisfaction her response to them. As she took her seat, she faced them and informed them in Spanish that she was happy to join them on the flight.

Looking back to how she handled the racial epithet on our street, it was what was best for me as a still-developing person. My mother's reaction gave me two important gifts:

- She showed by example that dwelling on hateful messages is a waste of energy. Her own life had taught her, a dark-skinned woman with kinky hair, that there are too many other mountains to climb to spend time responding to every foolish act.
- Even more importantly, she did what every mother's love does: she protected me from internalizing harmful ideas. This concept is so crucial, and today many are doing a deep disservice to children by indoctrinating them with ideology.

THOUGHT CONTROL

Compare my mother's approach to what is quickly becoming the dominant way we teach children about race today.

In 2020, the book *Antiracist Baby* by Ibram X. Kendi hit number one on *The New York Times* Children's Books Bestseller List. The publisher lists the book as appropriate for ages 0–3. Kendi's book advocates that we should start teaching children as young as a few months that someone is either "racist or antiracist."

The book then lays out nine steps for achieving the goal. One step is raising awareness of skin color and further teaching children to be aware that skin color comes with privileges or the lack of them. This is illustrated by a white-skinned child viewing a white-skinned child climbing up a ladder and obtaining a trophy, while the dark-skinned child climbs up a broken ladder.[9] The message is the darker-skinned child will not succeed because the ladder he must climb is different.

Kendi then goes on to encourage *babies* to notice(or parents to point out to their babies) "policies don't always grant equal access" and that "all races are not treated the same." What year was this book written? In 1961?

What kind of message is this for a child? How is a child supposed to interact openly and freely with the individual he encounters?

Kendi also suggests that children be encouraged to notice we are all human, that "certain groups" are not "better" or "worse" and encourages the antiracist baby to stay "curious" about

---

9   Ibram X. Kendi, illustrated by Ashley Lukashevsky, *Antiracist Baby* (Kokila, June 2020), pg 7–8.

people "to avoid presuming to know a person without getting to know them." All wonderful and true, yet it encourages seeing people as groups. One particularly disturbing illustration in the book shows "white" characters interacting with "black" characters in a patronizing way. It might be well-intentioned, but it overcompensates for presumed victimization, reducing the "black" character to child-like status.

It is a bad enough lesson for adults, but this is the starkly reductive premise at the heart of all of Kendi's writings. Spreading these ideas to children is unconscionable.

A child that young is unlikely to be able to comprehend ideas about race, "equity," and policy, but at some point in their development, the child will begin to understand what is being taught: to reduce people to their skin color and heritage. Is that something that benefits them and sets them up for a better future?

Children for the most part remain oblivious to these categories unless prompted by adults to make something of it. In my own family there are dark- and light-skinned people. As a child in St. Croix, it never occurred to me to notice that my cousin playmates were dark-skinned. Similarly, during my time in the Dominican Republic, I did not think twice about being the darker skinned one among my cousin playmates there.

Teaching racial reductionism to a child is sinister. I acknowledge that some who spout "antiracist" dogma may think they have good intentions. But pushing adult political agendas on children is evil because it sacrifices the child's development to satisfy the ideological needs of adults. Children need to be children, to grow up with a sense of wonder, and to be happy people, and not to be recruits in someone's ideological army.

Self-assured about their own righteousness, racial ideologues want to capture children as young as possible, giving their investment in human infrastructure a longer time to pay off. It is infinitely sad to me that so many individuals are being taught to love and nurse their grievances, instead of developing a capacity for positive, productive lives. We are sacrificing futures to satisfy the political yearnings of ideologues.

And we are beginning to reap what we sow.

During the height of Black Lives Matter protests in the summer of 2020, SkyNews of Australia captured a group of young people of all skin colors stopping at a diner in Washington, DC.[10] Confronting people in the outside seating area, they pumped their fists and screamed in the faces of diners. Their goal, if they could be said to have had one, was to insist that the diners affirm that black lives matter.

Why they believed declarations coerced under those circumstances had value is baffling and more than a little disturbing. But these are the results when you teach children to relentlessly focus on race through the lens of victimization.

Clearly these young people had not been taught the values of wisdom and moderation, which would have enabled them to

10   "Black Lives Matter Protesters Confront White Diners Outside DC Cafe," SkyNews, August 26, 2020, video, 2:28, https://www.skynews.com.au/world-news/black-lives-matter-protesters-confront-white-diners-outside-dc-cafe/video/a48a8cf0e94c400cfccc152be1f3cb1.

make reasoned arguments for their cause. Instead their minds were saturated with self-righteous anger born of an ideology repeatedly pressed upon them, that America was a place of powerless victims whose only choice was to tear down society. This ideology is an effective way to conscript an army to carry out a job, but not a way to raise reasonable citizens.

This is not to say that the death of George Floyd that set off scenes like this was not horrific. Peaceful protests and calls for police reform were entirely understandable and justified. Unfortunately, most of the protests were not focused on specific and workable reforms, but instead on violent rioting and demands to defund the police and replace them with community-based enforcement.

We are in for more of the same, or worse, if ideas like Kendi's maintain influence. We are doing children a deep disservice when we teach them that everyone is either a victim or an oppressor, and that your race automatically determines your status in that hierarchy. Telling a child who identifies as black that they are a powerless victim of white supremacy sets them up for failure, not success.

Unpacking this even further, the whole premise could never work because it is rooted in a contradiction. We are supposedly trying to teach about racism to end racism. All this does is more deeply embed the concept of race into young consciousnesses. In many ways, this goes to the heart of the matter: instead of working toward the dream of the original civil rights movement of a colorblind society, we have doubled down on labeling and emphasizing race.

According to Kendi, to be colorblind is to "ignore what is in front of you." I disagree. It is true we cannot avoid seeing skin color, but we do not have to assign meaning to it.

Just as disheartening is depriving children of the opportunity to learn to think for themselves when they are told what to believe by way of ideology. When children see that we trust them to work things out for themselves (like my mother did), they exercise the part of their mind that has the capacity for wonder and independent thought. That muscle atrophies when handed a ready-made ideology.

Racial dogma shrinks the world and produces young people who are angry and less productive. It encourages navel-gazing and wallowing in emotions of pity. When you repeatedly tell people that their agency is limited, you end up with people screaming in incoherent rage at bewildered diners, and nothing changes.

A BETTER WAY

What should we be teaching our children?

I remember attending an event in Houston where Hillsdale College President Larry Arnn spoke about education and the stages of a learner's development from childhood to early adulthood. He had a lot of intelligent insights, but it was one simple statement that stood out to me in particular.

He said the mission of Hillsdale was to offer education to everyone who wants to learn because "people wish to live human lives."

It reminded me that both progressives and conservatives would likely claim that both wish to see people live out their lives in their full humanity. The caveat, however, is in how each perspective defines living a truly human life.

The classically conservative view is that the purpose of life and education is to develop the spiritual and intellectual tools to become a creative and productive human. Another way to express this is: humans need to gain the skills and values that promote agency and control over one's own efforts and outcomes. This is true liberty and defines what constitutes a life well-lived in the classical liberal sense.

On the other side of the aisle, progressives focus more on the temporal and material. Education is a prerequisite to a job in order to earn nice things. According to this perspective, students with lower socioeconomic backgrounds are assumed to be at a disadvantage. Statistics do bear that out, but the question becomes how to overcome it.

The progressive solution puts an intense focus on data and abstract groupings, and that can lead people to overlook the human person in front of them. Instead of seeing the capacity for individual development and teaching the tools necessary for a creative, productive human life, the emphasis is on what the person lacks and how to compensate for it rather than constitute the person.

Taken to the extreme, this can turn into a misplaced focus on outcome gaps, leading to Kendi-style ideas of reducing everyone to either a racist or antiracist. Ironically, a big part of the reason for poor outcomes are the very ideas being pushed by ideologues. They reject curricula grounded in the teaching of mathematics, natural science, music, and most of all, properly teaching children to read. This is something even schools with meager resources used to do.[11]

Instead of using this proven education method, students now learn from materials elevating values contrary to human flourishing. A focus on developing the virtues of wisdom, prudence, moderation, and citizenship is the solution, but students are stuck with curricula rooted in modern psychobabble and trendy educational theories.

While there is some evidence that income differences do have an impact on educational outcomes, the solution is not to remind students of their disadvantages. It is to treat children as beautiful humans with a natural curiosity and an innate ability to develop their minds.

At its most fundamental, education should be about helping children find the *good*, the *true*, and the *beautiful*. This concept of human life is a thread that runs through ancient philosophy and religions. There are those who call this education out of step, or even racist, but it is a far superior guide to teaching children than racial ideology.

Broadly defined, the good is that which is ethical; the true is that which is logical; and the beautiful are those ideas and images that aspire to their highest form. The wonderful thing is that children are natural learners and hunger for these concepts.

We should shine a light on the best our culture has produced

---

11   Thomas Sowell, *Charter Schools and Their Enemies* (Basic Books, 2020).

and hold up positive examples to encourage children's natural inclinations for more goodness, truth, and beauty. We need to avoid emphasizing division and ugliness, because it obscures their vision of what can be achieved in life.

REAL DAMAGE

The damage being done to children from the relentless focus on race is not theoretical. Often the consequences are hidden from view, but occasionally a story will break through and reveal what is happening.

An example of this is a young man named "Jeffrey," a cousin of Itabari Njeri, American Book Award winner and author of several books on multiethnic identity. Njeri describes her cousin as a Ricky Nelson look alike but with an intense desire to prove he was "the baddest n- on the block."[12]

The insistence came from his community, a pretty rough and tumble part of Harlem, and Jeffrey was eager to be accepted, even to destructive ends. Reading Njeri's account, one is left to wonder what Jeffery could have achieved with his parochial school education if others had only accepted all of him and not made him feel as though he had to emphasize the narrative of trying to be the toughest in the neighborhood.

Another example of pushing race narratives on young people occurred in 2020, when parent Gabrielle Clark filed a lawsuit against a charter school in Las Vegas, Nevada, alleging that her

---

12   Itabari Njeri, "Who is Black?" *Essence* 22, no. 5 (September 1991): 64–67, 115.

son William was asked to declare in class his race, "gender," religion, and sexual identity.

This is bad enough, but it was taken a step further, and the students were required to next attach labels like "oppressor" to their declarations. William, who identifies as biracial, refused to call himself an oppressor. For his lack of participation in this absurd exercise, he was given an F. Even worse, he was threatened with not graduating.

That a young person would be put in this position is obviously provoking. It raises a question too. What could those students in the class have been learning instead? Increasing math or language skills, learning to make logical arguments, or focusing on a positive role model from history all come to mind. Using precious classroom time dissecting a person's "race" is immoral.

I met Gabrielle Clark briefly at an event in Houston, and I applaud her willingness to take a stand. It is going to take many more people to stand up against racialization and for common sense to stop this massive ideological educational experiment from being conducted on our children.

CRITICAL RACE THEORY

Critical race theory (CRT) suddenly started getting a lot of attention in 2020. Ever since then, the general public has been wrangling over what it is, and whether it is impacting curricula or not.

Many ideologues understand that this is a profoundly unpop-ular philosophy with parents of all colors. In response, it has become popular to claim that CRT is not infiltrating down to the classroom, that it is a rather harmless theory taught in graduate schools and conservatives are using it to scare parents and voters.

Frank McCormick, a high school history teacher from Waukegan, Illinois, wrote an opinion piece for the *Chicago Tribune* that sheds important light on this issue. In his piece entitled, "I Am a Teacher, and Yes, Critical Race Theory Is in Your School," McCormick says that teachers deny CRT's influence because many do not understand it all that well themselves.[13] He also notes that the words critical race theory do not have to be used specifically for it to have an impact on what is being taught.

CRT can get slippery depending on who is defining it, but McCormick goes to the heart of the matter, saying it rests on two premises. One is that racism in America is "not aberrational but normative." In other words, racism is pervasive and hugely impactful, not something now at the margins of American life.

The other premise is related to the first: America's institutions remain inherently racist, just as they were in the past. As McCormick sums it up, CRT claims that racism "permeates our modern sociopolitical fabric."

One of the key underpinnings of CRT is that truth is not objective, but instead sits on the foundation of "lived experiences."

---

13 Francis McCormick, "Op-ed: I Am a Teacher, and Yes, Critical Race Theory Is in Your School," commentary, *Chicago Tribune*, November 8, 2021, https://www.chicagotribune.com/opinion/commentary/ct-opinion-critical-race-theory-schools-20211108-l77lxp4w5bgoljetdg42iv3dy4-story.html.

This essentially means the above premises cannot be falsified because they are rooted only in subjective viewpoints.

McCormick states that you will not find CRT mentioned specifically in teacher manuals or curricula, but that it is "a theoretical framework and tool" that lies behind many of the ideas that do get expressed in schools.

In other words, the two premises are widely accepted as true, and then that "truth" is applied in the practical teaching of children.

McCormick gives some examples of how these ideas get expressed in schools:

- Claiming that a school is systematically racist and labeling policies as oppressive
- Demanding that teachers use activist language because that is the only way to get rid of supposed institutional bias
- Forcing staff professional development to participate in trainings that "interrogate" race and power
- Lesson plans that require students to similarly "interrogate" race and power dynamics in the classroom

The piece ends with a paragraph directed at his fellow teachers and it perfectly captures my own thoughts on this subject:

> More important, teachers, do not use the sacred power and trust bestowed upon you by parents to impose this worldview upon their children. You are educators, not activists, and if you think you are the latter, you should reconsider your post.

Many racial ideologues claim that when parents oppose CRT, it is a smokescreen, and what they really desire is to cover up America's troubled racial history. Some activists may truly believe as much, but I believe many use it as a tactic to provoke a response, and then label the response racist.

If the riotous school board meetings around the nation about CRT that followed are evidence, it would appear an overwhelming majority of parents are not interested in these cynical games or ideologies. They simply want what most parents want: a good, solid education for their children, for their children to do better than they did, and for their children to be happy.

What parents oppose is forcing all subjects, history included, into a distorting lens that claims racism is inherent to America and as such inescapable. We only have to look at our amended Constitution to know that this is an incredibly one-sided story. A fair-minded appraisal of our Constitution and its history tells the story of a move away from a troubled racial history, and toward a transformation into equal protection for all enshrined in law.

CRT and its associated praxes are methods for constructing a false reality and making slaves out of an entire generation. I will have more to say about history in Chapter 5, but first a look at higher education and how it helps fuel terrible ideas like CRT.

CHAPTER 4

Academia and Race: No Dissent Allowed

"This is slavery, not to speak one's thoughts."

—EURIPIDES, GREEK TRAGEDIAN

In the summer of 2015, I was an adjunct professor of English at a community college in Houston. I had been there only a few weeks and was rekindling a professional relationship with a colleague from my teaching days in Qatar who identified as black.

One day we were chatting and the subject of Bruce Jenner came up. Jenner had recently come out as a woman and adopted a new name: Caitlyn Jenner. This conversation was taking place at the height of affirmation in the mainstream media of Jenner's announcement.

Also at this time, scorn was being heaped on a woman named Rachel Doležal for claiming a black identity despite apparently being born to two "white" parents. Doležal had been a well-known social justice advocate, a well-liked professor of black studies, and had even become chapter president of the NAACP in Spokane, Washington, before the controversy forced her resignation.

I shared my confusion with my colleague about the degree of contempt and hatred being directed at Doležal. For one thing, I was not completely convinced that everything about her heritage was being reported. It seemed unfair to be so sure of her ancestry when genealogy is often complicated.

But even more, I wondered about the contrast in societal reactions to these two stories being given prominent play at the same moment. Jenner had changed "gender" and was celebrated unequivocally in the mainstream media. Doležal had declared a racial identity rooted in her own feelings and was rejected with great anger. It seemed contradictory to me. Why was one considered changeable and the other immutable?

I thought I was asking a reasonable question about something worth exploring. My colleague did not. The conversation ended on a low note, but I would not realize just how low until a few days later.

That was when I learned that a suggestion had been made to the administration that perhaps my contract should be reconsidered. Even more than my suggestion about Rachel Doležal, my colleague expressed upset that I was refusing to identify myself as black.

Unfortunately, in today's highly politically charged academic environment, this could not just be two colleagues with differing views. It could not be left alone, because this was about race, and I was picking the wrong team (or more precisely, refused to pick a team).

To me it was a death knell to any hope for full-time employment. As an adjunct professor, my employment was on an as-needed basis.

It is difficult to articulate the range of emotions one experiences when someone tries to malign you for simply honoring all parts of your heritage. I filed a complaint with the college, and eventually received a tepid letter acknowledging the situation but holding no one accountable for suggesting I should be let go for my views about race.

I could not help but think that if I had made a similar suggestion about someone who identified with one of the protected classes, I would have been fired immediately (and rightly so).

After receiving the letter, I visited the diversity officer at the college. He acknowledged that it was wrong for someone to use race to suggest I was not qualified to teach. He also dismissed my concerns with the statement, "we are all multiracial when you think about it," essentially agreeing with my point of view.

Yet, he stood behind the official reaction of the college, which was you kept the job so no law was broken. I requested that the colleague at the very least receive sensitivity training, but this too was met with incredulity. It seems that in academia, only one side is held accountable.

In the end, I could see the writing on the wall. Any future promotions would be tough in that environment given the lingering resentments. By then, it was midway through the fall semester, so I finished it out and then handed in my notice.

This was not my first experience with the power of racial orthodoxy and leftist ideology in academia.

I share the above story and the ones that follow to give an inside look at the atmosphere in academia. I do this not to complain, but to witness to the decline of freedom of thought, and to show that academic culture is in the grip of racial and leftist ideologies.

Witnessing to this is particularly important in our current environment, where some try to claim that critical race theory and other ideologies are not the driving forces in academic culture. These voices say critics are exaggerating for the purposes of gaslighting and political manipulation. My interactions with academia over the years tell a different story.

A WINDING JOURNEY THROUGH ACADEMIA

Back in the mid-1990s, I did my undergraduate work at the University of the Virgin Islands, a historically black college and university, initially majoring in journalism but switching to speech communication and theater after my first semester.

It was there I got a taste of what a real classical liberal education could be. My courses consisted of literature, history, economics, statistics, anthropology, philosophy, linguistics, rhetoric, classical literature, and early Greek theater.

I loved the classes in my major. We were a small group, and our method of learning and debate was Socratic. Many of my classmates were from the British islands and had received a primary and secondary education based on the British model of formal education. This model allowed them to choose an academic path (instead of a vocational one) after sitting for a battery of tests in core subjects.

This meant that these students had demonstrated the ability and motivation to get the most out of a liberal arts education. They were sponsored by their respective governments because they had survived this process and were selected to attend the university. My classmates were intellectual forces in the making given their proven educational excellence.

Seeing what learning and intellectual life could be at its best inspired me to create a vision for my own future, and I looked forward to the day I could continue my education at the graduate level. But first I worked for a number of years in the travel and leisure industry in a variety of roles. Then came 9/11 and my trip to the Middle East. In the years after, I dabbled in travel writing and teaching language arts, but my drive for more education never went away.

In 2010, I came to the Washington, DC, area, finally ready to pursue a master's degree in English and sharpen my skills for teaching writing and literature. I chose George Mason University in Fairfax, Virginia, with high hopes for replicating and extending the experience I had at the University of the Virgin Islands.

Unfortunately, the reality would not match those hopes.

At George Mason, much of my teacher preparation centered on what I was told were best practices for teaching the language arts. Those "best practices" turned out to be a bunch of progressive theories about how to teach writing.

A few examples:

- Emphasizing emotional expression over grammar and traditional tools, the latter being deemed too prescriptive
- A focus on teachers being "de-centered" and essentially leaving the child in charge of his own education in the name of a more "authentic" expression
- Personal identity was always an emphasis. I can still clearly remember one professor standing in front of a seminar pontificating that "personal identity *is* political."

Theory always seemed to take precedence over how to best get children to practically improve their writing skills. There was also a great deal of jargon and a preoccupation with concepts like postcolonialism, or a critical study of the impact of colonization on colonized people.

My research professor who was apparently a math genius but gave that up to focus on postcolonial literature had us read Rudyard Kipling's *Kim* through the lens of oppression. Our only graded assignment for the semester was a twenty-five-page paper discussing that oppression.

A course on Arabic literature focused on emerging writers from the Middle East/North African region. One in particular was a young woman who used full frontal nude displays of her body on social media to address the oppression she suffered as an

Egyptian woman. (She and her family had eventually been forced to flee the country for their safety.)

Perhaps it was possible to get some insight from this kind of education, but I failed to see how it was helping us figure out how to better equip our future students with the language skills they would need to be successful in life.

It was also around this time I encountered Derrick Bell's critical legal theory (somewhat erroneously cited as the basis for much of what would become CRT) and Paulo Freire's *Pedagogy of the Oppressed*, a foundational text in teacher preparation programs and the forerunner to critical teaching for social reform. So much of the academic theory was reminding educators of what their students *lacked*. I often wondered what could be accomplished if we saw students as individuals full of *potential* and were trained to bring their innate abilities to the surface instead of viewing them as helpless victims to be saved.

I am not opposed to healthy debate on what may genuinely help children in lower socioeconomic circumstances, but it seemed no one ever came to any practical conclusions on how to improve teaching methods.

For example, I remember an inordinate amount of time being spent in our seminars on whether to teach grammar explicitly or not. This taste for nonstop theoretical debate seemed as unquenchable as it was pointless. No consensus was ever reached, and it gave me no direction on how to better help students in a classroom.

It also became clear that graduate-level academia is enamored of anything supposedly "new." If you can come up with something that sounds different, no matter how convoluted, it is the path to advancement and sometimes notoriety. This contrasted sharply with my previous more traditional liberal education, which was rooted in the idea that the wisdom of the past shapes and forms you, not the other way around.

That more classical vision was no longer to be found in places like George Mason, at least as far as I could tell from my graduate program. It seemed that all the brainpower was focused on finding a new twist on the latest fashionable theories. And nothing was (and still is) more fashionable than theories on race, intersectionality, critical theory, and other ideas grounded in leftist ideology. The formula was to use one of those abstract theories and add some new twist. This is what drives the increasingly bizarre academic concepts that seem to have no touchpoints with the real world. Academia is an isolated audience, putting on performances for each other.

Undergirding many of the fashionable theories coming out of academia is the absence of objective truth. Post-modern thinkers such as French philosopher Michel Foucault (1926–1984), who theorized the relationship between language and power, are especially influential. According to Foucault, language and meaning are in a constant state of flux. More importantly, however, those in power will "organize language, in such a way to maintain power." We see this in the continual creation of identity groups through the language of critical theory and the influence these groups exert in social policy.

These performances have a serious purpose, however. These new theories generate prestige, and that means money. Universities want to have professors and graduate students doing "cutting-edge" research, or at least work that can be perceived that way. In the humanities, this seems to mean taking the approved ideology and creating some even more abstract spin on it.

One way to sum up the problem in academia is to note that the jargon word "problematize" has become popular. The goal of education is no longer to get at the truth and to find happier and more productive ways to flourish as human beings. Now the aim is to problematize everything and interrogate it as such at the intersection of two mutually inclusive domains. Of course, the academics who create the problems also put themselves in charge of fixing them. It is an insane feedback loop that never goes anywhere.

After my George Mason experience, I went back to the Middle East in August 2012 to teach at a newly established community college in Qatar. For the most part, politics and race did not enter into the equation there. Many of the students and professors came from conservative Muslim societies, and it was a different atmosphere than colleges in America.

Despite my not great experience at George Mason, I eventually decided to return to America, and in May 2014 I entered a doctoral program in English at Indiana University of Pennsylvania (IUP).

What I did not understand going into my education at the doctoral level was how much of it was about learning to talk and write like an academic. You discourse in what sounds like English, but it might as well be an entirely different language.

You learn this language not to get better at becoming an educator or to train others to be better at it. You learn it so you can communicate with other academics.

While I do remember at least *some* of the time being spent on interesting discussions, there was much too much time wasted on a plethora of critical pedagogies about identity creation and analysis.

Even the single required course on classical rhetoric, which included a substantive reading list of the early Greeks from Homer to Cicero, could not resist encouraging a "(Re)Turning to Aristotle" or calling for "The Revitalization of Civic Discourse in American Life," with the inevitable slant for teaching public discourse for social change and "performing identity."

Another course centered entirely around French sociologist Pierre Bourdieu and his concept of the unconscious production and reproduction of power. His theories posit that this power was deposited in a person, guiding that person's thinking and being, and ultimately impacting the individual's agency in society. Somehow, this was supposed to influence pedagogy when teaching the oppressed, but it was never clear how. Some of my professors would gush in apparent hero worship over what these gods of the field had produced. At times, the adulation had a genuinely cultish feel.

As a whole, the key takeaway of our indoctrination was that we would go out into the world to teach children about what they lacked. We would give them tools to help them understand how oppressed and impoverished they were and how the world was set up to be systematically unjust to them.

Not much emphasis was put on giving learners the tools of independent thought that could show them a way out. If independent thinking and effective skills actually started showing results, the whole narrative edifice of oppressor-victim would crumble.

Despite my reservations about what was being taught, I completed three semesters with a 3.87 GPA and then put together a qualifying portfolio, the equivalent of oral exams used by some doctoral programs to determine a prospective candidate's advancement to the dissertation level. I was rejected as a candidate. I appealed, and again I was told no.

It is possible that I was not advanced based solely on a judgment of my portfolio. Given my GPA, I had felt I had demonstrated the capacity for advanced work. Furthermore, none of my professors had given me reason to think otherwise. But given that my views were not aligned with the prevailing orthodoxy of academia, a doubt burrowed into my brain. Had I been rejected because of my apparent discomfort with the progressive context?

Part of the reason we are so split on race and ideology as a culture is a lack of trust, and that is rooted in a perception about lack of fairness. Was I truly rejected because my portfolio did not warrant being advanced, or was it my contrarian views on race, education, and rejection of the oppressor-victim model? There is no way to know for sure.

My individual disappointment is relevant only to me, but I do believe there are many who hold what are now deemed "unacceptable" views and who are asking the same kind of questions. It eats away at our social fabric.

There is a solution, however. Return the academy to its true purpose: expanding human potential rather than examining every aspect of intellectual discourse through the filter of irrelevant racial classifications. End ideological litmus tests and simply judge the talents and merits of the individual. If we are going to have fairness and justice in education, colleges must be held to these standards or higher educational institutions should be defunded from receiving federal dollars.

After my time at IUP, I found myself at the Houston community college where I became embroiled in the controversy mentioned at the beginning of this chapter. For me, it served as the culmination of a journey into the increasingly radical heart of academia. Each step of the way, from George Mason to IUP to Houston, I found the ideology more out in the open, and less tolerant of any form of dissent.

I wish I could say that I thought things were improving in academia, but if events reported in the media are to be believed, those hallowed halls are becoming increasingly treacherous. A quick review of some recent stories reveals an increasingly authoritarian approach to any opposition:

- A renowned University of Chicago geophysicist was invited and then uninvited to give a prestigious lecture at MIT because he rejects essentialism, believing instead that people (and his students in particular) should be treated as individuals and on the basis of their work.[14]

---

14   Dorian Abbot, "The Views That Made Me Persona Non Grata at MIT," opinion, Wall Street Journal, October 29, 2021, https://www.wsj.com/articles/cancel-culture-college-mit-dorian-abbot-university-chicago-representation-equity-equality-11635516316?mod=trending_now_opn_1.

- Harvard suspended a notoriously anti-woke stance academic despite his own challenging upbringing based on a several years old, questionable accusation of inappropriate sexual advances.[15] This despite demonstrated success educating students from low socioeconomic backgrounds.[16]
- In an article for *Atlantic* magazine, John McWhorter's survey of 445 academics revealed a widespread fear of expressing controversial views. He also shared snippets of emails he received from other academics showing self-censoring for fear of expressing "wrong" opinions, a pressure to "toe the ideological line," and a statistics professor's concern for discussing the fallacy of assuming disparity equates to discrimination.[17]

This is where we are now. What if all that intellectual energy were used to find ways to create a truly better world? Surely it would be more productive for peace and happiness than our unrelenting pursuit of more theories about oppressors and victims.

The spotlight our culture places on historical divisions and horrors is a primary reason we have come to such an impasse. So it is to history we now turn.

15   Peter W. Wood, "Harvard Cancels a Black Academic Who Debunked Woke Orthodoxy," New York Post, March 25, 2022, https://nypost.com/2022/03/25/harvard-cancels-a-black-academic-who-debunked-woke-orthodoxy.

16   Ben Casselman and Kim Tankersley, "Harvard Suspends Roland Fryer, Star Econommist, After Sexual Harassment Claims," The New York Times, July 10, 2019, https://www.nytimes.com/2019/07/10/business/economy/roland-fryer-harvard.html.

17   John McWhorter, "Academics Are Really, Really Worried About Their Freedom," The Atlantic, September 1, 2020, https://www.theatlantic.com/ideas/archive/2020/09/academics-are-really-really-worried-about-their-freedom/615724.

CHAPTER 5

What Is History For?

"If you think you have it tough, read history books."

—BILL MAHER, AMERICAN COMEDIAN
AND POLITICAL COMMENTATOR

What we choose to remember as history does not change the past, but where we choose to focus our gaze does change the present and future.

Some might say that we should not choose what to remember, we should just recall the facts. I agree that facts should be the basis of history, but it must be acknowledged that the collective stories we tell about our country always involve *choosing* what to focus on and what to ignore.

To remind ourselves that history involves choice is simply stating a fact. Even the best and most studious historians can only examine a tiny fraction of everything that has ever happened. For non-historians (pretty much all of us), this is even more true. There is only so much time available to us, and we have lives that must be lived forward.

In order to make an intelligent choice about what stories we give the most weight, we need to ask ourselves a fundamental question: *What is history for?*

The dominant academic and media culture in America has a default answer: To remind ourselves of all our most terrible past shortcomings and to flagellate ourselves for it. And then to use that past to remind ourselves of how terrible we still are.

Of course, it was not always like this. The media, books, and schools used to tell an overall positive story about our history. The negative was not ignored, but the overall portrait pointed to our founding, our freedoms, and our mission "as the last best hope on earth."[18] Part of its purpose was to inspire us and to pass solid civic values on to the next generation.

Of course, those who told our nation's stories were not always completely fair, and they had their blind spots too. It is good that we have mechanisms to correct history as needed, and to give as complete a picture as possible. The negative aspects have their place.

However, telling the truth is not the equivalent of putting an exclusive spotlight on our failures. It is possible to acknowledge the shortcomings within an overall aspirational story.

---

18   Abraham Lincoln, "Annual Message to Congress—Concluding Remarks," Washington, D.C., December 1, 1862, https://www.abrahamlincolnonline.org/lincoln/speeches/congress.htm.

It is a fallacy to think that if the "warts" of our history are not emphasized, we are somehow being dishonest. That argument could be flipped on its head. Is not the de-emphasizing of America's history of political freedom and economic success just as dishonest, if not more so?

The choice we are making now is to maximize the stories of past racial oppression and tensions in the United States. Would it not be better to ask ourselves what a constant underscoring of America's past injustices is doing to our future? The incessant drumbeat produces two outcomes: people tire and disengage or they become disillusioned, or worse even, destabilized. Eventually a significant part of the body politic is going to become infected with the idea that America is irremediably evil, and always has been. What kind of citizens are formed when a country's story about itself is so negative?

There is a better way. Every American of every color can be told a truer story about our country's aspirational heritage. Each generation indeed needs to be told that this country was founded as an experiment, and it is up to us to preserve the integrity of the Union that was handed down to us. This should be the foremost goal of the stories we tell about our past.

Some will no doubt see any optimistic framework for American history as propaganda. But a positive view of American history, even regarding race, is not only defensible but also reasonable.

In fact, I would argue that a relentless focus on the flaws of the American experiment is the real propaganda. An insistence on racializing everything is what gives us a distorted view of who we have been, who we are, and who we can become as a people.

Here is an illustration of what I mean:

It is a fact that the United States Constitution condoned slavery. I know of no reasonable person who would not want that as a part of our historical knowledge of ourselves.

But it is an equally true fact that our amended Constitution not only specifically outlaws slavery, but also codifies that every American citizen shall be treated equally under the law.

How did this change happen? Part of the answer is, of course, the history of the Civil War. But on a deeper, philosophical level, it is because America has been an aspirational country ever since Thomas Jefferson wrote in the Declaration of Independence that we are all created equal.

The fact that we have not always lived up to those aspirations is part of history, but so is the reality that we have successfully struggled to make our country a "more perfect Union." This idea of always becoming *more* perfect is so fundamental to our concept of America, it is in the very first sentence of the U.S. Constitution:

> We the People of the United States, in Order to form a more perfect Union, establish Justice, ensure domestic Tranquility, provide for the common defense, promote the general welfare, and secure the Blessings of Liberty to ourselves and to our Posterity, do ordain and establish this Constitution for the United States of America.

I am not suggesting that the Civil War or the Thirteenth Amendment have been completely erased from our textbooks or our cultural memory. However, I think any fair-minded person would agree that the loudest voices increasingly focus on the hurts and violence of our past more than the healing and forward movement that have occurred.

An example of this is the almost casual way the term white supremacy is used in today's discourse. This phrase should have a specific historical meaning. Factually, it can be taught as a major factor in slavery and its aftermath. It is a term that can be accurately used today to apply to fringe movements with support at the extreme political margins.

But the words white supremacy have been repurposed to supposedly describe a fundamental reality of today's America. Just like "racist" is thrown at people who are no such thing, white supremacy is now being used to paint everyone with the broadest possible brush.

The phrase is used so indiscriminately that it is now thrown not only at people with so-called white skin but also at people of black and brown for little more than their political affiliation. This was the accusation by an *LA Times* columnist about California gubernatorial candidate Larry Elder because of his Republican politics.[19]

Today some schools are teaching that America's true founding was 1619. This is categorically false, with an argument that is woefully weak and without any coherent premises. If 1619 is the origin, where is the instrument that effected that origin?

---

19   Erika D. Smith, "Column: Trump Branded the GOP a Party of Racists. Elder as Standard-Bearer Won't Help," *Los Angeles Times*, September 15, 2021, https://www.latimes.com/california/story/2021-09-15/larry-elder-california-recall-loss-shows-gop-weak-racism.

(Where is its Declaration of Independence? Where is its Congress?). It is all tenuous connections and jamming facts to fit a narrative. The 1619 claim has no document or act that reveals the true founding of a country.

It is also worth asking: What does trying to force a negative foundation narrative inspire in its future citizens who are in classrooms today? Whatever the faults of our founders in 1776, they gave us something to aspire to, not something to drag us down.

When we hear politicians and media figures make the deceptive argument that newly passed voting laws are the equivalent of those from the Jim Crow era South, what does that do to bring us together? When we are told that white supremacy still reigns like it did in the days of slavery just with better camouflage, how does that help us build a culture of trust and a stronger society?

All of these claims are rooted in cynical lies based on using emotional words ("Jim Crow," "American founding," "white supremacy") in ways that completely twist their original meanings. Yet these are the stories we are telling ourselves now.

THE IDEA OF REPARATIONS AND HISTORY

One issue that tends to surface these dysfunctional views of history is the idea of paying reparations to African descendants of slaves. I find this another area where the radical claims of racial ideologues are exposed as contradictory on a practical level, and are also wrong as a matter of principle.

Once thought to be politically impossible, several major Democratic presidential hopefuls supported the possibility during the 2020 primary campaign. Even Joe Biden has sent ambiguous signals that he is open to reparations since taking office. The issue no longer seems as theoretical as it once did.

Let's first examine the practical problems with reparations. Remember back to Chapter 2 where we discussed how challenging it is to determine heritage past a certain point, even with DNA. Recall also that there can be no specific objective definitions for declaring someone to be a particular race. All these fuzzy definitions around race and color surface again when you begin to sort through the complexity of how reparations would work practically:

- I was born in the United States to a descendant whose ancestors were slaves in the Virgin Islands when it was a Danish possession. Would I qualify? Technically, would it not be the people of Denmark who would owe reparations to me?
- For that matter, would I be required to pay reparations, as my ancestry also includes European descent through my father? Or would we simply erase and overlook this part of me?
- How specifically would reparations be paid out?
- Have some people already been paid in the form of affirmative action programs? What about those who have been receiving, some for generations, government benefits such as welfare and disability? If so, how do you decide who is still owed what?
- Would descendants of slavery who have achieved academically, in commerce, still be entitled to reparations? For example, would a millionaire who built a successful business or a university president qualify?
- With the lack of clear, objective definitions of race and pin-

pointing heritage, would it just be based on what someone claims? What specific criteria would you use to qualify or disqualify that person?

These are just a small handful of complications; the list could be much longer. Once you drop down off the philosophical plane and descend into applied realities, the actual complexities are exposed—yet another example of getting tied into knots in race debates that are both impractical and contradictory.

Opposing reparations goes beyond just practical matters, however. Reparations also symbolize one group of citizens extorting another group of citizens. I acknowledge that many people who would support reparations are not thinking like extortionists, and I also realize the statement probably strikes some as too harsh a description. But is it inaccurate to say activist voices that make the loudest arguments for reparations would never be quite satisfied? When the focus remains on past oppression, the temptation will always be to demand more.

We need to think carefully and be honest about the relationship that reparations would establish between fellow citizens. It is asking one set of citizens without personal guilt to pay another set of citizens. Doing so would further entrench the oppressor-victim dichotomy, with a power dynamic similar to extortion.

THE REPARATIONS I AM FOR

If America is going to pay any form of reparations then this should be a solid K–12 education, the kind that instills character *and* enables that person to go out and create, innovate, and build a life around whatever it is that person does well.

So the best reparation is a solid education in developing reading, writing, and reasoning skills irrespective of zip code, tax base, or "race" of the child. Most reparations plans call for money to be spent in the trillions. A better use for that money would be for schools to provide students with a strong foundation, a classically liberal education. There was a time in this country when we did exactly that.

Another reparation we particularly need is forgiveness. I realize some will call that naïve, but it is the only way to truly heal. As I have stated several times, I do not think it is healthy to identify by race. But for those who choose to do so, to remain angry about the past is destructive to their own lives. I grieve for people trapped in this damaging mindset.

Slaveholders and the Jim Crow era establishment are no longer here to deprive anyone of life and liberty. We are citizens in the land of the free, the freest of all the places I have seen. Blaming your current fellow citizens is counterproductive because it holds them accountable for something they never did, and it robs you of your happiness.

It is also a mistake to believe that leveling the playing field by bringing one group down or another up based on outward characteristics will make outcomes always equal. Such an approach only leads to an equality of poverty. We are as good as we challenge ourselves and are challenged to be. No one wallowing in self-pity will suddenly stop because everybody around them is now wallowing in pity. Misery may love company, but it will not create positive change. Upward and onward, without looking back or trying to get others to fix your problems—that is the way forward.

To lift burdens, there is no better path than true forgiveness for past wrongs. This does not mean forgetting or not honoring your ancestors. It does mean honoring their sacrifices by committing to do better, focusing on the future while letting go of historical resentments, and focusing on tomorrow. Always choose to move forward and avoid the lure of remaining stuck in the past.

BLACK HISTORY MONTH?

Setting aside a month out of the year to highlight "black" achievement is a well-intentioned idea but one that supports the belief that we must continue to classify and divide ourselves by race.

It is another example of trying to free America from any remnants of racism by continuing to underscore "race" as fundamental and, in my view, reinforcing what we claim we want to eliminate.

There is value in telling of the contributions of slaves, the formerly enslaved, and their descendants that were undeniably minimized for a significant part of American history. And not just minimized, but sometimes misrepresented. How we retell these stories now, however, constitutes the difference between building collective pride or group grievance.

For example, a Clemson University intellectual property lawyer and patent expert has documented the contribution of slaves and free blacks to America's economic boom in the 17th and 18th centuries. During this period, patent protection was extended only to citizens of the United States. As some inventors were slaves and not recognized as citizens, patent law did not include them.

Slave masters often intervened (sometimes in good faith but not always) to secure the patent instead. In one case, a patent for the cotton scraper was denied the slavemaster since he was not the actual inventor.

But in another well-documented case, a free black man invented the four-poster bed frame. Misunderstanding patent law, he decided to partner with a citizen who was white, and who was then granted the patent for the invention. In yet another case, the inventor of a propeller for shallow water steamboats also was a slave and so could not secure a patent because of his status; but he went on to market his invention anyway. Interestingly, all three of the actual inventors went on to become extremely wealthy.

The nuances of these stories matter. Notice how each revolves around patent law and slavery, but all have important differences in details. Too many times, stories like this are all lumped together in condensed thirty-second "moments in black history" prevalent on the airwaves every February. The entire story cannot be told in neat little packages.

We can tell these stories anytime, and in full, as part of the American story that we all share. Instead, when filtered through the official designation of Black History Month, and poorly so, it implicitly ties an entire group of people to this exploitation.

Tell the facts and specifically who did what. If the racial perceptions of the time were part of the story, go ahead and identify that fact too. But stop making it a black story or a white story and make it an American story.

The problems go beyond how stories are presented. Just the idea of having a bracketed-off month sends the message that somehow the part of history involving those with African heritage is somehow separate.

At the beginning of the chapter, I noted that what we focus on in the past shapes our view of the present. If we are separating history by color, it logically follows that we will use that past to keep telling separate stories.

It is sad and ironic that we do this because the true story of America is much more layered, much more nuanced, and much more fascinating. We have overcome so much division and melded so many different people from so many countries into a vibrant democracy and a land of opportunity. Imperfectly to be sure, but better than any other form of government in human history.

There is also another level of exploitation of Black History Month. Many of the most powerful people and institutions in our country are happy to show how supportive they are of the month's theme, but one can be forgiven for wondering whether the support is rooted in a facile cynicism.

There are the photo opportunities for unprincipled politicians to show their support of Black History events in February, and the corporate communications announcing their community initiatives. Perhaps some of the sentiments are sincerely held, but one gets the feeling that it is more about votes, marketing, and not being attacked on social media. Public support of Black History Month then is, well, very public, and perhaps without the purest of motives.

I think of my view of Black History Month in the same way I think of my personal history. My individual history cannot be set aside in parts divided. I am a product of my past and my ancestors in a way too beautifully mixed to ever pull apart into component pieces. I believe the same about our country. Black history is part of the overall American story, characterized at times by struggle and by no means sinless. Tell it all the time, every month of the year.

WHAT ABOUT JUNETEENTH?

In 2021, the US government created a law establishing a new federal holiday declaring June 19, or Juneteenth, a day of national celebration. Juneteenth is a celebration of the day slaves learned of their emancipation, a celebration that was localized to Texas for a long time but eventually grew to become more widely known.

I first learned of Juneteenth while a graduate student and remember thinking that January 1—the date of Lincoln's Emancipation Proclamation—would be a more appropriate date than June 17. It seems to me celebrating the emancipation of the slaves on the first day of the new year is not only more historically accurate, but would set the tone for recognizing the passing into history of slavery, a significant American story, and not only about the states where Juneteenth was originally celebrated.

I recognize that the Emancipation Proclamation did not in fact free all slaves, but it was the turning point that explicitly made the Civil War about not just preserving the Union, but also freeing slaves.

Indeed, there are debates about what Lincoln said he would do to preserve the Union. But would it be illogical to deduce that a man who started a political career on an anti-slavery platform, publicly supported the Thirteenth Amendment, and advocated for the extension of the franchise to freed slaves intended to retain the slave economic system? To think otherwise is to misinterpret the nuances of artful rhetoric.

The first day of the new year is more appropriate for a day of national reconciliation, one that is already spent happily and celebrated and shared by all Americans of all skin colors.

I fear that a separate Juneteenth day could turn into a day of separateness and of scorn for one another instead of a day of harmony and reconciliation.

4 GUIDELINES FOR TEACHING HISTORY TO CHILDREN

History is complicated for all of us, and with growing minds we need to be especially aware of how we teach it. Here are four guidelines we should always keep in mind, no matter what month we are in:

1. **Are we being age appropriate?** For children in elementary and middle school, the emphasis should be on an almost journalistic approach: who, what, when, where, and how. Facts about what happened with very little interpretation, and certainly no complicated ideology layered on top. As

they grow into high school, introduce controversies and differing opinions in an even-handed way.

2. **Are we always asking ourselves how a child is benefiting from the history we are teaching?** A limited time to teach history always necessitates choices on what we teach and why. We should always tell the truth, but this does not mean elevating the bad over the good. We can and should choose to amplify what will best inspire happy and productive citizens.

3. **Are we reinforcing separateness or unity?** The story of racial perceptions in America is one of change, and mostly for the good. In 1864, slavery was still legal in fifteen American states. In 2008, a blink of an eye later in historical time, a multiracial man who identified as black became president and was re-elected for a second term. While I personally could not support his politics, I could appreciate how perceptions had changed, and I admired that about our country. It is an exemplary story of moving toward a more perfect union.

4. **Are we taking the right approach?** One of the problems with the discussion of most hot topics, and race in particular, is that we do not know what we think we know, and too many of us are repeating talking points filtered down into society through the media or textbooks putting forth revisionist history and cleverly spinning facts. If we are going to honestly teach about America's racial past, the solution is to teach the *history* of debates over race, instead of a single angle rooted in a specific racial ideology.

Of course, history is the big picture when it comes to race and its impact. But what about at the ordinary, daily level? What does a relentless focus on race do to us as individuals?

CHAPTER 6

Is Race Making Us Paranoid?

"Let me never fall into the vulgar mistake of dreaming that I am persecuted whenever I am contradicted."

—RALPH WALDO EMERSON, AMERICAN
ESSAYIST AND ABOLITIONIST

Sometimes it is not the big, loud, political stuff but the small daily interactions that add up and begin to wear us down.

This calls to mind for me a small incident from an ordinary evening at home. I had invited two friends from church in the hopes of starting a Rosary prayer group. This was at the height of the riots following George Floyd's killing, and a few of us wanted to come together to stand on a street corner among the protestors and pray. We were meeting at my house to get the group started.

The first friend arrived and said one of my neighbors had

eyed her suspiciously as she exited her vehicle in front of my home. Soon after, the other friend arrived and related a similar incident.

What ensued was both of them discussing what they might characterize as "what it is like walking in the color of their skin." I had been privy to this topic of discussion numerous times before from others. Still, coming from these two highly accomplished, successful professionals with a bearing projecting nothing less than attainment, I was perplexed.

None of my neighbors had ever made me feel unwelcome, nor had I ever heard or witnessed anything that would lead me to believe a neighbor would stare suspiciously at someone based on skin color.

I should also note that I live in a very diverse part of midtown Houston. My neighbors reflect a variety of ethnicities, mixed marriages, and orientations. The neighborhood also is very walkable so we get quite a bit of foot traffic, and as you might guess, those walkers are a diverse group. It seemed highly unlikely to me that one of my neighbors would find the sight of these two accomplished women as misplaced in any way.

A far more probable explanation to me was perhaps it was an aloof passerby who would appear standoffish toward anyone, regardless of color. Or perhaps the person had looked at them with no ill intent at all and the glance had simply been misinterpreted.

I do not want to automatically discount the experiences my friends had that night. To them it was quite real, and to be fair, I was not out on the street with them to witness anything directly.

Still, this very ambiguous interaction ended up consuming our evening on my patio under a beautiful night sky.

Being the hostess and hoping we would eventually return to our original purpose for coming together, I let them vent. (I also think people deserve to be heard when sharing their honestly held views, even if I disagree).

Thankfully, we also engaged in some conversation about moving forward. One of the women has two college-aged sons. She shared how they often remind her not to lead with race, i.e., refrain from the temptation to default to making everything about race. She also expressed that the generation of her sons, coming up as they did the benefactors of an integrated society, is our best hope.

Still, as I pondered the events of the evening later, I was saddened for those who feel trapped in these categories. It is to such an extent that we think we are becoming mind readers, interpreting each other's thoughts and motives—and in the worst possible light. This was only one small incident, but one illustrative of my point nonetheless. Unscientific, unfounded ideas about race have burrowed deep down into our souls and into our hearts, making us distrustful of one another, and maybe even a little irrational.

As a thought experiment, what if we presumed my friends were right and that a neighbor was staring at them with suspicion, sending a signal that they were not welcome? What would be the better response?

Ignore it and let it go. I refer to this as my "Yo Mama Joke Rule."

During my teenage years in New York, "yo mama" jokes were not uncommon. I do not know if folks still engage in this oratorical art form anymore, but back then it was a bit of a cultural phenomenon. Sometimes it was a playful game between friends, where the idea was to one-up the other person by coming up with the better insult about the other's mother. But there were times when it would be taken quite seriously, especially if you were interacting with rivals and trying to provoke a response. A joke cutting too close to home could turn into a physical fight even among friends.

I remember witnessing these confrontations on occasion and being absolutely bewildered by the intensity of the emotions that were sometimes aroused. Why on earth would anyone let someone who says something about their mother—who the person does not even know—get someone angry enough to risk injury in a fight? The response never made any sense to me. Walk away, do not give it oxygen.

In an analogous way, why let a stare or a thoughtless remark influence your actions? If you think a person is making a thoughtless judgment based on your skin color, do not reward them with the favor of your energy. Doing so would be like wasting your time fighting with a person who told a thoughtless yo mama joke.

Does this mean we overlook *overt* attempts to denigrate our dignity? In these cases, what matters is how we respond. We are human, we have feelings, and some of us love to have the last word, but not every stimulus warrants a reaction or bears repeating. Of those times when a response is warranted, may it always be measured, appropriate for the moment, and grounded in dignity, both for you and the other person.

In your daily life, for the sake of your own mental wellbeing, give people the benefit of the doubt. We rarely can know what anyone else is really thinking. And even if that person is thinking bad things based on skin color, do not drain even one second of your own energy worrying about it; it is simply not worth responding to.

WHAT ABOUT THOSE RACIST REPUBLICANS?

In my own experience, those often stereotyped as racists are not. I can say this as a woman with brown skin who lives in Texas and is active in local Republican politics where I am a chair of my precinct. I am also active at the national level, showing up for conservative causes including the annual Conservative Political Action Conference (CPAC).

I can honestly say that I have never been made to feel uncomfortable because of the color of my skin at these events. I also see many others like myself, every skin tone and heritage participating, and I have never witnessed a discriminatory act or word toward them either.

This could be because truly no incident has ever happened in my vicinity. Or it could be I did not notice any such incident because I do not wear "antiracist" lenses set to look for racism and therefore do not pick up on it if it happens. Either way, I am happier and healthier for it.

Of course, my more left-leaning friends are cynical of my activism in the Republican Party and my attendance at CPAC events. And depending on whom among my liberal friends I am talking to, it is not unusual for me to hear snide remarks about "what they *really* think of you."

Sometimes the person will go on to imply conservatives are tolerating me because they want votes, cynically using me and others as poster children for diversity in the Republican Party when they actually do not care. I have even heard "just wait till all of that tap dancing is not enough."

There is an assumption embedded in these comments I find a bit insulting. For starters, my liberal friends and acquaintances, and some family members, presume I could only participate in conservative politics as an unwitting dupe who is being manipulated by others. It could not possibly be that I am fully aware of what conservatism stands for and so I consciously made a decision to exercise my civic duty accordingly. (We will address this issue more fully in the next chapter.)

The other underlying assumption is that the Republican Party is rife with racists and hateful ideas. When I read mainstream media coverage of Republicans (I deliberately avoid broadcast media and increasingly some print legacy media too), particularly over the past few years, I am not surprised that many people have this impression.

Like sex, race sells. The topic gets clicks and eyeballs to tune in. I know something about how the media works having been a publicist first at a number of boutique public relations firms and then media relations manager for an international hotel and cruises corporation for some years. It was my job to literally come up with ways to direct the consumer gaze toward our product and then go out and feed media gatekeepers—both national and international—with the words I wanted them to say about our product.

If you ever watch one of those common social media montages of "analysts" that claim to be reporting news, you will notice they all say the same exact things across times and outlets. They use the same words and phrases, often verbatim!

These "journalists" are not even bothering to *at a minimum* take the numerous press releases coming across their stations' news desks and make the words their own. This is just one example of how the media is not about objectively going in search of facts or doing their best to provide a balanced view of reality. There are always exceptions, of course, but for the most part our media are now more akin to propagandists.

The media want clicks, viewers, and the advertising dollars that follow. It is lazy and cynical reporting that makes us paranoid about our fellow citizens. I tell you all this to suggest that following the impressions given to you by the media is not a good way to the truth.

However, here is the good news: you can free yourself from this race porn and resulting paranoia by committing to never pre-judging or categorizing anyone based on media stereotypes. The people I meet in conservative circles care about the freedom to use their inherent agency to make a living, to do so in an economic environment supportive of those ends, and to express themselves politically and creatively. They also want the same possibility for all their fellow citizens, regardless of their heritage, because they understand it is what leads to human flourishing in the truest sense.

A good rule for all of us in every social situation, whether it involves politics and race or not, is to treat every person we interact with as a singular individual. Refrain from assuming you know exactly what a person is thinking unless that person tells you. And do not go on to guess why they think it. Listen to the person and make the effort to not parse their every word for ill intent.

Active listening and charitable interpretations in every conversation will take us a long way down the road toward happier individual lives and a more inclusive and productive society overall.

THE ASSUMPTION THAT "MINORITIES" CAN'T BE RACIST

As you know by now, I am not fond of the fact that many ideologues toss the loaded word "racist" at every opportunity. Nor am I fond of label words like "minorities." Nonetheless, this is the language and framework set up by those who I wish to challenge, and so I am going to play by their rules for just a minute in order to point out their contradictory claims.

A common refrain we hear from ideologues is "oppressed minorities can't be racist." As with so many of their language ploys, they start by creating their own definition of racism to justify this claim. Racism according to "progressives" is prejudice *plus* the power to act on it. Therefore, because oppressed people do not have power, de facto they cannot be racist.

This argument has multiple fatal flaws. If you label and treat people differently because of their outward characteristics, that is racist, regardless of how much power you have. It also is a very narrow definition of power. If power is the capacity to direct or influence behavior or an outcome, anyone who can bully or hurt anyone else has power. And that is all of us. (This progressive definition of racism also serves to reinforce the characterization of "minorities" as helpless victims with no agency).

Perhaps a person with a multiethnic background can see that racism can cut both ways a little more readily. Many of us have had experiences of being bullied for merely being who we are.

I think back to a formative experience in high school that ended up with my removal from the school. During several years there, I had been mercilessly bullied by other girls whose skin was darker than mine and whose hair was coarser and kinkier. This group of girls had decided I *thought* I "was better" than them because of my lighter skin and finer hair.

In another incident I was on the subway with friends on our way home after school when I was brutally attacked by another gang of girls, motivated by the same animus. It was unprovoked, and as you would imagine, extremely unpleasant for me. Not long after this incident, I transferred to a neighborhood high school for my senior year.

One of the lessons of these stories is that prejudice about skin color could come from any direction, and that is true enough. But this is not the main lesson I draw from those experiences.

The larger lesson is this: how infinitely heartbreaking that our preoccupation with race and skin color creates conditions where we hurt each other and waste our potential clinging to identities based on superficial appearance.

I do not know or cannot recall whether those girls at school were punished or expelled, but if so, what a squandered opportunity for them. Also sad was the absence of self-awareness in those young ladies. As I write this I find myself wondering if any of them ever moved toward becoming productive and happy people.

Not everything I experienced on New York City's MTA was traumatizing, however. I will never forget the day early in my freshman year as I was boarding the A Train to school when a dark-skinned girl approached me and with an enormous smile on her face she told me her name and asked me for mine. We have remained friends ever since that day. Goodness and grace also come in all skin colors.

Incidents like the not-so-positive one on the train are a reminder of the costs we pay for the lie that is race. Rather than continuing down the path of hurt, pause and ask ourselves:

- What is the measurable gain from centering race in the daily goings-on in our lives?
- What is the cost to our souls? To our children? To our inheritance?

Are we a freer people now since news media, advertising, corporate branding, public—and increasingly private—education have "opened our eyes," empowering us to shout from the mountain tops at every possible moment the accusation of "racist," real or perceived? Or is this freedom turning us into slaves to paranoia and fear?

CHAPTER 7

Race and Political Polarization

"Can't we all just get along?"
—RODNEY KING, AMERICAN SURVIVOR OF EXCESSIVE FORCE

When race is injected into politics, nobody wins. It is a tactic serving only to exacerbate existing disagreements, create more division, and work against healing historical tensions. As is the case in every area of life, we would be better off colorblind, operating from the unifying aspiration of an American identity spoken into being by the Founders.

One of the most outspoken critics of a colorblind society, Ibram X. Kendi, says in *Antiracist Baby*, "you cannot ignore what is in front of you." But this is because they see it so, treating skin color as though the amount of melanin in one person's skin is something of a calling card, provoking the same reaction in everyone to whom it is presented. Other critics of the concept of a colorblind society argue practices such as redlining, refusing financing to a person due to their zip code, would continue unaddressed if race is not considered. Here, activists may have a valid point about narrow-minded banking policy. But does this give credence to the assumption that the only people living in low-income areas all comprise the same group?

Seeing politics through the lens of race also works to reduce the acceptable range of political choices, at least for some. It is taken for granted among most cultural commentators that if you identify as black or "minority," you only have one home in American politics: the Democratic Party. This supposed truth is of course false, and there are many examples of exceptions. Nonetheless, the idea holds broad sway.

There was a revealing moment giving credence to this view during the 2020 presidential campaign when then-candidate Joe Biden was a guest on the popular *The Breakfast Club* radio show hosted by a man who refers to himself as Charlamagne tha God.

Biden said if someone was having trouble deciding whether to vote for him or for Trump, then they "ain't black." This was a good illustration of taking for granted a block of voters, as Biden was essentially saying that no one who was truly black could consider voting Republican.

Some leveled the accusation that this was a racist statement, but I disagree. It would be hypocritical of me to throw that word around casually when I criticize many racial ideologues for doing that exact thing. However, it was a telling moment of pandering to a voting bloc that the Democratic Party continues to assume is in their back pocket.

To my ear, I heard Biden saying, with a wink and a nudge, "Everybody knows you won't vote for those racist Republicans, right?" Politics is a rough and tumble business with plenty of amoral tactics, but cynically sorting people by race only deepens our divisions, and I found this comment to be undignified. Imagine the outcry if a Republican presidential candidate had made a similar statement presuming the support of a white constituency.

While much less pronounced in the Republican Party, there is a worrying trend at political rallies. Even here, we are seeing the use of identity politics to show support for conservative candidates. At 2020 rallies, you could see signs and T-shirts proclaiming, "Asians for Trump," "Women for Trump," "Blacks for Trump," and so on. While I understand this is meant to combat the impression of monolithic support for the Democratic Party, it is reinforcing exactly what should be combatted. Conceding to identity politics is the wrong path; better to stick with reason, ideas, and policies for creating better economic and political conditions.

Even so, it is the Democrats who seem to be doubling down on the idea of racial identity and skin color as a fundamental part of politics, and this is revealed in both overt and not so overt ways.

For example, Valerie Jarrett, a former advisor to Barack Obama, stated on a CBS morning program in 2020 that the nominee for vice president should be "a woman, a person of color" because doing so would "send a very important signal."[20] We heard a similar refrain when it was time to fill a vacated seat on the

---

20 Valerie Jarrett and Jamal Simmons, "What Do the 2020 Democrats Have to Gain from Super Tuesday?" *CBS This Morning*, March 3, 2020, video, https://www.cbsnews.com/video/what-do-the-2020-democrats-have-to-gain-from-super-tuesday.

Supreme Court in early 2022. The presidential administration vouchsafed that the spot could only be filled by a woman and she would be black.

The mainstream media for the most part did not question this limitation on the potential candidates. Instead, they went about their usual business of tea leaf reading (and beta-testing in front of the cameras) from among three women most likely to be the nominee.

These were Leondra Kruger, J. Michelle Childs, and Ketanji Brown Jackson. A fourth candidate, Anita Earls, was sometimes mentioned, but one gets the feeling she probably never really stood a chance because she did not look sufficiently black in her pictures. This to some extent may have applied to Kruger and Childs as well. It is sad that not only do some politicians feel the need to declare litmus tests based on race and sex, but then one suspects they go even further by asking who meets those criteria sufficiently based on nothing but optics.

There are other examples of this that grab a small amount of attention but fly under the radar. It has been reported that Barack Obama was close to marrying another woman besides Michelle, except choosing Michelle was "politically expedient" and offered a better image for his career. Had Obama married a "white" woman, would he have been perceived differently? The answer is almost for sure yes, and that says something about the optics and politics of skin color.

Skin color optics are also a problem that has plagued Kamala Harris, as many who identify as black find it laughable that she is being passed off as someone who personifies the community.

It was not long ago in politics that we played a simple game of group proportionalism, where there was an effort to have some representation by race in high-profile positions. But that is no longer enough. We are now in the era of full-blown skin politics by shades of skin color.

This reminds me of the infamous "brown paper bag test" in the post-Reconstruction South. This was a real thing. The idea was that no one who was darker than a poke sack could be accepted in elite circles.

Now somehow, just like with the "one-drop rule," we are regressing. We are repeating history, but now going to the other extreme. The solution is to stop letting skin color play any role in politics at all.

An eye-opening book on how we arrived at the point where "identity" plays such a huge role in our current politics is Mike Gonzalez's *The Plot to Change America*. The first half of the book offers extensive insight into how a "Hispanic" voting bloc was constructed and then instilled with grievances to validate claims for compensatory justice.

It is a long and somewhat complicated story, but the condensed version is this: building on the justified claims of historical marginalization from community advocacy groups, and fueled by significant funding from organizations like the Ford Foundation, a slow but intentional plan coalesced Spanish-speaking people into an aggrieved Hispanic category.

My father and his fellow citizens from the Dominican Republic would not have understood this lumping together of all

Spanish-speaking people in the Americas as Hispanic. Their identity was in their specific culture and nationality, not in an umbrella category that was constructed for cynical political reasons.

The same blueprint is being used to create a pan-ethnic Asian identity or Middle Eastern/North African identity (MENA). All this is occurring with the implicit support of the Census Bureau and its National Advisory Committee (rebranded in 2012 as the National Advisory Committee on Racial, Ethnic, and Other Populations). There is seemingly an endless appetite to find more and more ways to divide us and to encourage people to take up the cause of an aggrieved victim. As Gonzalez's book shows, there are powerful and well-funded groups behind these political movements.

THE SUMMER OF GEORGE FLOYD

The terrible summer of 2020 only highlighted and exacerbated the folly of mixing race and politics.

Without question, the video of George Floyd's killing was absolutely horrifying. It cut to my soul, and the look of derangement in the police officer's eyes as it happened was a terrible thing to see.

The aftermath of the release of the video revealed the extreme dysfunction of our institutions and culture. Instead of attempting to focus on justice and healing, the actions of the media and activists maximized conflict and rage.

The escalation began with a cynical and amoral media that continued showing the video over and over for days. From a journalistic point of view, it could be argued that airing the video was initially necessary to show what happened. But the repeated showing of it again and again for days revealed a media that reveled in the higher ratings and increased clicks.

There seemed little interest in balancing the needs of reporting what happened against sensationalistic, provocative coverage that was rousing an angry mob mentality. Stunned by these scenes, I sent emails and called some of these media outlets to ask them to demonstrate restraint for the good of these communities about to explode (not to mention George Floyd's family and friends). It was an attempt to do something to quell the violence, but having worked with the media during parts of my career, I should have known it was going to be a futile effort. At a certain point, the media had to realize the relentless playing of the video was striking a lit match near dry tinder, but this did not slow them down.

Of course, what happened next was rioting, looting, and chaos in several cities. Sadly, this violence hurts people in lower socio-economic conditions and the businesses that serve in these communities. There were some denunciations of these actions, but in many quarters of the media and among some politicians, the actions were portrayed as understandable and legitimate protests.

It was stunning to hear the media continue to refer to the "mostly peaceful" protests as the mayhem and burning continued. They helped light the match and then they half pretended nothing was burning.

The summer of 2020 also gave a big boost to the movement

known as Black Lives Matter. Let me affirm unequivocally that of course they matter. I also understand why at this moment those who identify as black wanted this emphasized.

But it seemed to quickly morph into something else. Suddenly it was acceptable for non-African politicians to don kente cloths when any other time cries of "cultural appropriation" would have filled the airwaves. Corporations, major sports leagues, and especially politicians suddenly got religion in this area. The point did not so much seem to be to find justice or workable solutions for those in communities riddled with crime and poor education. Instead, it seemed about who could send out the most social media posts decrying racism or touting their latest anti-racism training.

There were also unclear demands that got a lot of coverage, including calls to "defund the police." For a few, the phrase seemed to mean reallocation of some police funding for social services, which if done in a smart way could potentially make sense. At least it was something that could be reasonably debated.

But those voices were drowned out by louder, more radical ones. Many seemed intent on using defund efforts to punish all police with slashed funding. In the most extreme versions, some called for 100 percent defunding, effectively abolishing the police. Fuzzy concepts about community self-policing were proposed as a replacement. There were even some calls to abolish prisons too.

Fringe ideas are not new, of course. But the media covered them seriously, which gives fantasies about abolishing law enforcement the appearance of credibility. No matter how outlandish the idea, as long as it was seen as supporting the "right" side of our political divide, it was treated with kid gloves. Adding to the problem is that sane people are afraid to speak out against insane ideas for fear of being labeled a racist in the press or piled on in social media.

Today's outlandish idea can also become tomorrow's reality. Take, for example, some medical protocols instituted during the COVID-19 pandemic.

Several states, including New York, Minnesota, and Utah, adopted policies that gave preferential status to "people of color" over "whites" for COVID treatment. For example, New York said that race would be a factor in who could have access to the breakthrough antiviral Paxlovid. If you were deemed "nonwhite," that alone was enough to be eligible for treatment, no matter your age or risk factors. So-called whites would have to prove some additional risk factor to gain access. Were these hospitals testing for one drop of African blood, or were they operating solely on the presumption of skin color? One has to wonder.

The argument for these preferences seemed to be that COVID took more of a toll in some communities than others. That may be true on its surface, but those kinds of statistics are created because individual outcomes are aggregated. For treating the individual in front of you, the only thing that should matter for allocating scarce treatments is that person's specific risk factor.

Of course, politics always involves money, and who controls that and how it is spent is one of the tactics used in these ideological wars. Perhaps one of the most frightening tactical ideas in recent years is an idea put forth by a pair of Columbia University sociologists. Known as the Cloward-Piven strategy, this husband and wife team proposed flooding the welfare system to the point it—and the urban governments' hopes of sustaining it—would implode under the weight of the number of recipients.

This would then force a policy of universal basic income to address the certain resulting crisis. In fairness, these sociologists floated the idea as a way to address income inequality among *all* ethnic groups. However, one gets the sinking feeling that besides being ruinous economically, it would not be long before racial ideology became part of this overall strategy.

The Cloward-Piven team expressly stated its wish for "bureaucratic...and...fiscal disruption in local and state governments...to deepen existing divisions among elements in the big-city Democratic coalition."[21] It would appear that to a certain degree, this strategy was partially implemented during the COVID pandemic. COVID was used to justify record unemployment benefit payouts, rent moratoriums, loan forgiveness for certain "minority" farmers, and the beginnings of what might be complete student loan forgiveness for all.

I fear we could see these types of policy preferences grow in all areas of American life, unless enough people begin to see through the manipulation. The history is there to see how this plays out. After the race riots in northern cities in the late 1960s

---

21   Richard Cloward and Frances Piven, "The Weight of the Poor: A Strategy to End Poverty," *The Nation*, May 2, 1966, archived at https://web.archive.org/web/20111124045536/http://www.commondreams.org/headline/2010/03/24-4.

and 1970s, "temporary" benefits became permanent, and money poured into these devastated communities but somehow ended up lining the pockets of "community activists" more than the people the funds were supposed to help.

To a degree, the same occurred after the death of Michael Brown.[22] And early in 2022 we learned of the millions raised funding the lifestyles of Black Lives Matter founders. If one thing has become clear in the smoke-filled haze of racially based uprisings, it is the money pouring into these devastated communities—and into the pockets of race hustlers—in the aftermath of these crises. It seems like COVID and other crises become useful in racial politics to the degree it allows the money spigot to flow untempered. The trend toward treating these race issues with money is hard to stop once that door is opened.

It is in this environment that emotional pleas turn into political currency, that claims of victimhood become a shield from having to use reason to defend ideas. Instead of expressing and defending ideas, people censor themselves for fear of being labeled a racist. On the other end of the spectrum, some use emotionalism to indulge in worshiping their feelings and to avoid the burden of having to formulate reasonable arguments.

As a country, we need to take a deep breath before we self-implode.

---

22 *What Killed Michael Brown*, directed by Eli Steele, written by Shelby Steele (2020; Man of Steel Broductions).

CHAPTER 8

Are We Worshiping the God of Ideology?

"Whatever your heart clings to and confides in, that is your God, your functional savior."

—MARTIN LUTHER, GERMAN THEOLOGIAN

In the summer of 2020, pop culture megastar Beyoncé released a visual album on the streaming service Disney+ called *Black Is King*. I cannot say with certainty her exact artistic intent, but the popular website The Ringer posted a rapturous review by Taylor Crumpton. Beyoncé's performance "reinforces the ancestral lineage of Black people as *divine beings* born from the natural and spiritual forces of the universe."[23]

In many ways, I find this a sad attempt at waxing poetic, and the

---

23 Taylor Crumpton, "Glory B: Beyoncé, the African Diaspora, and the Baptism of 'Black Is King,'" The Ringer, August 4, 2020, https://www.theringer.com/movies/2020/8/4/21353713/beyonce-black-is-king-african-diaspora-orisa-oshun, emphasis added.

sort of facile rhetoric that arrogantly assumes it can uplift a presumably downtrodden people who need a collective uplifting. As to equating black people with divine beings, I am reminded of the great chain of being and similar attempts by medieval thinkers to equate themselves with the angels.

If Crumpton is simply asserting black lives are indeed as worthy as the Europeans who did omit them for their medieval hierarchy of matter and life, I can sympathize without endorsing how he says it. It is nonetheless a troubling choice of words and seems to imply that merely being black moves one to the head of the "divine being" line, second only to God.

Whatever Crumpton's precise point might be, something else seems to be taking place in our culture, of which this visual album is just one small sign. Idolizing skin color is insidiously inserting itself into all aspects of the culture. We noted in politics that it is now used as an overriding and determinative factor in judicial appointments, even to the highest court of the land.

But it goes well beyond politics. Corporate advertising seems excessively committed to finding the exact right representation to prove their woke bonafides. Social media activists appoint themselves to say who can speak for a community and who cannot. Companies and nonprofits alike pour lots of energy into putting on what appear to be little more than diversity displays via their websites.

This mindset is even infiltrating churches. I myself witnessed firsthand obvious skin color proportionalism in determining the makeup of committees and councils in my parish.

All this focus on the idolization of outward color creates a crude caricature. It is akin to the "I have black friends" to supposedly prove you are not racist, while proving you are. How is exploiting skin color to showboat diversity based on outward characteristics any different?

We need to reject this now. We cannot raise a generation where skin color is the first aspect we notice about a person, and where the color of one's skin is the person's most important quality.

What is going on that would cause the racial ideology of mere mortals to begin taking on the qualities of a religion?

Humans are natural worshippers. We are also moral creatures, and traditionally what we worship also gives us our ethical bearings. If we begin to lose this anchor, the majority of us will not stop worshiping or looking for strong moral guidance. We will simply look for a center and a compass elsewhere and, sadly, in all the wrong places.

My purpose is not to evangelize, but to analyze. Some readers will have religious beliefs, some will have secular beliefs, and I am not trying to change yours. I do, however, happen to view the world through a Judeo-Christian morality.

I do think it is worth analyzing the impact of moving away from a tradition of objective ethical values to help understand why people seemed motivated to add a religious dimension to racial ideology.

Traditional religious beliefs create a relationship with God, and that relationship in turn provides a grounding for objective truth. Perhaps it is no surprise that the historical figures who most informed progressivism and activist ideology have been irreligious themselves. Karl Marx, co-author of *The Communist Manifesto*, famously called religion "the opium of the people." Friedrich Nietzsche (the son of a Lutheran pastor!) could be credited with letting loose ideas like "my truth" and other relativistic concepts into the modern world. He declared that "God is dead and we killed him." He considered Christian morality a form of "slave morality," essentially claiming that playing nice gets one nowhere. Jean-Paul Sartre, father of existentialism, further popularized and extended these atheistic concepts in the twentieth century, allowing for all this to run amok in higher "education."

Rooted in ideas like these, the "progressive" education agenda, with its relentless focus on race, "gender," and sexual orientation, has slowly and systematically eroded objective truth. The individual self and its arbitrary characteristics become more important than reasoning together toward truth. This in turn can tempt some to elevate characteristics like skin color into holy attributes.

Either by intention or instinct, ideologues exploit this where they are most likely to succeed: in the realms of race and guilt. When conflated the two become a manipulation, eliciting sympathy for the descendants of those trod upon historically, while also inducing guilt from present-day citizens who were yet to be born.

Just as bad, people are encouraged to wallow in victimization, and this also begins to take on a veneer of worship and mortification. When victimhood is held up as one of the highest values, it empties a person. Instead of a confident person endowed with agency, the person is diminished, reduced to little more than an empty vessel.

While I watched some of the rage-filled rhetoric spewed by many activists during the summer of 2020, it dawned on me that many did not seem to know who they were deep down. In the rhetoric, there was no discernable connection to God, no relationship to universal truths, and no sense that a life could be cultivated by leaning on a power much greater than oneself.

Ideologues often oppose even considering religious tradition, arguing the ideas were formed by "dead old white men," privileges "bourgeois values," and panders to "respectability politics." I never thought of the people who inspired Judeo-Christian thought and the foundational principles of this country as "white" men. Besides, I saw their descendants up close with my own eyes and can confirm, unequivocally, that they come in all sizes, shapes, skin and eye colors, and hair textures. All that matters are their ideas and their capability for critical thought; the color of their skin is irrelevant. I do find it depressing that these racial ideologues never seem to ask whether the values they so cavalierly reject might help them flourish more than the emotionalism, unhinged rants, safe spaces, false truths, and feel-good psychobabble they defer to.

That might sound like a stark assessment, but what is at stake are happier, healthier, and more productive lives. A life grounded in objective truth and morality, and a charitable interpretation of our neighbor, is a time-tested path to a life worth living. The wrong path is one rooted in victimization and the elevation of the individual to sacred status.

That is the road to folly and foolishness. It is like the folks who tried to build a tower to themselves, but ended with the divisive and chaotic Tower of Babel instead.

People will satisfy their impulse to worship one way or another. We need to stop indulging the temptation to worship ourselves and our outward characteristics and find our way back to truth.

THE NIGRESCENCE MODEL

The connection between the receding of traditional faith and the rise of ideology and "identity conversion" can be seen clearly in an influential theory and subsequent five-step model developed by the academic William Cross in the 1970s. It was during this time in the embers of race riots afflicting northern cities that theorists began calling for a black psychology to address problems specific to those communities, and to engender a black identity in those who had assimilated. The word *nigrescence* is French and loosely translates to the process of becoming black. The original model has been updated a few times over the decades and has had significant influence in many black studies departments around the country.

It is interesting that Cross himself describes the genesis of his theory happening only after a traumatic losing of his own traditional faith soon after arriving at college. The Nigrescence Model of Identity Development that he invented has the earmarks of a conversion, and in fact was also described by him as "The Negro to Black Conversion Experience."

What follows is an admittedly simplified version of each step in the conversion process, but it gives a sense of how the process becomes a quasi-religious experience where the initiate comes to "see the light" about being black in America.

In the original, pre-encounter state, the person does not realize that they are living in an assimilated state, one where they do not truly belong. Next they move to a stage of Immersion-Emersion, where they begin to wake up to the "truth" of their oppression, and intense feelings of anti-whiteness and a need for deep black involvement are unleashed.

Next, the person undergoing the conversion often joins black nationalist movements and begins to live out his newfound life of high racial consciousness. In some versions of the theory, this consciousness evolves further into multiculturalism. Whatever the specifics of each stage in different versions, what is fascinating is this idea that race can be a conversion experience. In fairness to Cross and others who collaborated with him, the aim of identity conversion, at least in part, addressed self-destructive behaviors and is said to have in effect helped some. Still, the theory developed by Cross is in essence the way to be indoctrinated into the religion of race and separateness. Interestingly, the model is known to have been adapted by theorists who have created other college "minority" studies programs in the formation of Hispanic, Asian, Native American, as well as gay and lesbian identities.

FREEDOM FROM ALL RESTRAINT

There is another mistaken notion that seems to undergird an I/me approach to society, and it centers around the true meaning of freedom. For much of the left, freedom means either a radical release from any restraint or the freedom to stamp out any ideas they dislike. These concepts of freedom not only contradict each other, they are both wrong.

Looking at freedom defined as a release from restraint (the freedom to "do whatever you want"), for example, many ideologues reject common standards of behavior as oppressive "white" values. Instead of reasoned debate about what moral principles and duties are in accord with a good life, they claim for themselves the right to dismiss all of it as tools of oppression.

There has also been an increasing appetite to annihilate any ideas these activists disagree with. Freedom here is defined as the freedom not to be confronted with any ideas that make you uncomfortable. Some even expect that the government should protect this "freedom" by insulating them from so-called hateful ideas. We recognize this as "cancel culture" where universities, corporations, and other employers are pressured to fire anyone who dares question the prevailing racial orthodoxy or even accidentally slips over a line defined by ideologues.

In one case, a Fordham University professor was fired after inadvertently confusing two black students.[24] He attempted to apologize, but that also was viewed with suspicion because his apology was deemed excessive and, thus, more evidence of his supposed racism. Nothing was going to be good enough for these true believers, and so the professor was sacrificed.

Moments such as these are scarily reminiscent of public shaming in Maoist China, where the only right answer was the answer

---

24 Joe Kottke, "Questions Remain After Sudden Termination of English Professor," *The Observer*, November 29, 2021, https://fordhamobserver.com/66231/recent/news/questions-remain-after-sudden-termination-of-english-professor.

the interrogators deemed correct. Except this is twenty-first century America. A particularly interesting footnote to the story: the impetus for the professor's dismissal was not the complaints of the two students he confused *but* of two other students bearing no resemblance who, presumably, thought it their duty to report the incident to higher-ups.

This is the sort of insanity that ensues when people become convinced that preserving their freedom means the stamping out of other people's freedom.

There is a truer way to look at freedom. One way is to use moral precepts to keep us from going down a miserable path. If we stay within those bounds, we have the freedom to flourish.

For example, people outside the Judeo-Christian tradition often think of the Ten Commandments as a list of rules meant only to restrain us from doing what we want to do.

This perspective is too limited. The overall context of all those "thou shalt nots" is to remind us to keep in proper and healthy relationship to God and our fellow humans. It reminds us to not damage those relationships. When we accept moral restraints, it creates more true freedom, because now we are free to stay in loving relationships with others, and to build happy and productive lives.

The Ten Commandments are one example; other traditions have similar moral precepts for the same function and purpose. We do not have to all agree on the exact source and detail of every rule, but if we are to live in freedom with each other, we must share values in common.

This is what the racial ideologues miss when they reject out-of-hand "bourgeois values" and "respectability politics." What they are really rejecting is the freedom to live together in healthy relationship. True freedom is the freedom to live a life in accordance with the true, the good, and the beautiful. It is not a freedom from all restraint, which leads to chaos and a kind of hell on earth.

It is not my intent to suggest that anyone who identifies by race does not have good ethical principles. Many do. What I am challenging is the slippery slope the loudest voices want us to slide down. On the contrary, privileging the idea that objective truth and values are tools of oppression can begin to seep deeply into the culture and sends us down a destructive path.

"CURRYING THE FAVOR OF 'WHITE' PEOPLE"

I need to address another tactic used by race ideologues to enforce conformity of thought: some like to accuse anyone who defends the traditional values of Western civilization as motivated by approval from "white" people.

According to this perspective, we live in a white supremacist society, meaning culture deemed "white" is supreme, the standard by which all other cultures are measured. They go on to say that some of us give in to this supremacy and cooperate rather than fight our oppressors.

We supposedly accept the "white" standard and thereby demean other cultures, like Black culture[25], or "Latino" culture,

---

25 Kimberlé Williams Crenshaw, "Race, Reform, and Retrenchment: Transformation and Legitimation in Antidiscrimination Law," *Harvard Law Review* 101, no. 7 (May 1988): 1331–87.

or "Asian" culture, or "MENA" culture. (Notice also that this viewpoint assumes that there is only one way to *be* any of those).

The exact wording of the accusation that some of us capitulate to "white" society varies, but I once heard it referred to as "currying favor with white people."

No doubt some will accuse this book of being nothing but one long attempt at currying favor. It is an effective tactic for putting someone on the defensive because there is no way to absolutely prove your own inner motivations. I could turn this accusation on its head and say to a race ideologue, "you are trying to curry favor with fellow activists." Rather than take the bait, however, I would like to suggest using this notion of "currying favor" in a positive way.

In living a life, almost everyone has some standard they use to judge their decisions and actions. So a good question for us all to ask is this: *Who or what are we trying to curry favor with?* Another way to think about it is this: *What are you using as the ultimate standard to judge your life?*

Many Americans are giving in to peer pressure by currying favor with politically motivated groups in order to gain acceptance and not lose status. The fear of social media attacks or losing reputation at work makes this pressure all the worse. This thinking can infect people on both the left and right. If that is you, then stop doing it. Then reflect on your true motivations: Who do you really want to curry favor with?

For me, as a practicing Catholic, I want to curry favor with Christ. For someone else, it might be Allah. For someone with more secular beliefs, it could be currying the favor of people you respect for their integrity and judgment.

The larger point I am making is this: we get so wrapped up in our own beliefs about politics and race and history that we lose perspective. We need to take time to reflect and aim toward a standard for our life that transcends our skin color and our politics.

Rightly understood, this idea of currying favor can actually help people escape the trap of a joyless ideology and start living a life with an eye upward and toward happiness.

CHAPTER 9

Creating a World Liberated from Race

"A journey of a thousand miles begins with a single step."

—LAO TZU, CHINESE PHILOSOPHER

For America's 240-plus years of existence, so much blood, ink, and sweat have been spilled because of false ideas about race. Yet no matter how many iterations we suffer through, and no matter how much improvement occurs, the shouting, turmoil, and conflicts never seem to end.

It is tempting to consider giving up and acknowledge that we are too deeply divided to ever heal or find peace on racial matters. But I refuse to go down without doing my part to preserve our great country.

Healing and change start with one person at a time. Individuals rid themselves of reducing their identity to their race. And the more people who liberate themselves, the closer we get to a race-free society.

Sounds good, but how can a person shake this idea of race so embedded in American history and so omnipresent in today's media? It helps to first recall all the contradictions that have been pointed out in the preceding chapters. Dethroning race is easier when we recognize that the concept crumbles under close inspection.

Race, biologically speaking, is a myth. This seems hard to believe but it is true: race is not real. Humanity is like the earth's ocean, as noted in Chapter 2. We can construct labels and name separate oceans, but in reality, it is one big continuous body of water. Humanity is also continuous; it is impossible to define where one "race" begins and another ends. This is a fact that is especially clear to anyone with a mixed heritage.

To say race is a myth is not to say discrimination based on skin color has not occurred. There is no denying that immutable characteristics like skin color and hair texture have played a huge role in American history. Even though racial categories are human constructs, people have made the effects real by believing in those categories.

Which brings us to the contradiction at the heart of so many of our current conflicts. Those with the loudest voices in our culture keep insisting the way out of our racial maze is to keep teaching racism. They say they will build up so much awareness and consciousness of outward characteristics for the purpose of transforming us into a society of perfect justice.

Unfortunately, that is magical thinking. You cannot incessantly focus on race and what separates us, and then expect that separateness to somehow cure what ails us.

The true cure is to train ourselves to let go of the concept of race altogether. To rid ourselves of racial strife, we need to de-emphasize race and the racial categories giving credence to that false notion so we can draw attention to what we hold in common.

This is not lying about race; it is 100 percent true: we all share a common humanity that transcends any constructed categories. This much I learned in my travels around the world and in the Middle East in the aftermath of 9/11, especially.

The best way to think of this is to remind ourselves that we truly are all people of color, and that we are not our race. This is just a fact. We say words like black, brown, and white, but each is just a lazy way to lump people together. Look at people individually and you will see an amazing array of hues—none an exact match of any other, and certainly no one that is the perfect archetype of those colors.

This is not some kind of warm, fuzzy interpretation designed to inspire (although I think it is inspiring). It is the complete truth and more accurate than any racial category. We are all people of color, full stop, period, end of sentence.

Even if you agree with this vision in the deepest corners of your heart, living out our convictions in an indifferent world can be extremely challenging. I hope I have encouraged you to strive toward living a race-free existence.

In 1971, the political activist Saul Alinsky wrote a book titled *Rules for Radicals*. I do not recommend the book itself, as for 50-plus years it has been a leftist manual on how to force change using cynical political tactics. But he does purport one rule I find useful: "The price of a successful attack is a constructive alternative." In that spirit, I have created constructive rules for getting past race and embracing our common humanity.

RULES FOR TRANSCENDING A RACE-BOUND WORLD

I have noticed that many of the most strident ideologues often seem angry and disappointed with life. They look miserable, and you know what they say about misery and company.

The best solution is to not meet negativity with more negativity; it is to meet darkness with light. To quote Martin Luther King Jr., "Darkness cannot drive out darkness and hate cannot drive out hate. Only the light can drive out darkness and only love can drive out hate."

With that principle in mind, here are the ten rules:

RULE #1: FIRST, DO NO HARM

In everything you do with/to/for someone else, strive to recognize the dignity of *that* specific person, not because of their race or their background, but for no other reason than that person is a human being. This does not mean we cannot call out wrong when we see it. But it does mean that when we do, we do so in a spirit of helping, not hurting or taking glee in our righteousness. The positive reverberations of this philosophy on the soul cannot be overstated.

Also, remember that at times you will fail at this, and some people will do or say things that make it particularly challenging to see their dignity. Commit to it anyway and do your best. It is transformative.

RULE #2: SMILE

There is a custom in the Virgin Islands where a person entering a room, an elevator, a government office, etc.; crossing paths with a stranger; or initiating any new interaction, must acknowledge everyone present with the appropriate greeting fitting the moment: good morning, good afternoon, or good night, and loudly so that the greeting is heard by all. Failure to do so would most certainly result in the offender either being ignored altogether or reprimanded harshly.

When I lived in the northeast part of the United States, I found this tradition did not really fit the region and was seen as counter to a cosmopolitan notion of good manners. In its place I made my greeting a smile, which is second nature to me anyway.

A smile will on occasion bring unwanted attention, but smile anyway and deal with those unwanted advances politely. Smiling is worth it. Science says it will boost your mood, helping the body release endorphins and cortisol for overall good health, including lower blood pressure, and nothing prevents or eases a tense situation more than a smile.

This is also supported by my Dominican heritage. Dominicans greet each other, strangers included, with a smile and a hearty "buenas!" With this kind of start to a human interaction, love is bound to pour forth.

RULE #3: TURN OFF THE TV AND UNPLUG FROM YOUR PHONE AND LAPTOP

It is important to stay informed of current events, but I think it is safe to say we have too much news coming at us from everywhere. Add in Twitter and other social media, and *presto!* A tsunami has appeared to keep us in a state of agitation.

Someone making a ridiculous racial argument on Twitter or in the "news" is intentionally telling only half the story. Instead of getting mad, why not turn it off? Go for a walk, read a book, go to church, visit your local coffee shop, or do whatever it is you enjoy.

When we stay plugged in too long and watch too much TV, we are putting our mental and spiritual health in jeopardy. Protect your mind and soul at all costs. Beware of others pulling you into negativity.

RULE #4: BE KIND AND LOOK FOR WAYS TO SERVE OTHERS

Rule #1 was about making sure we do no harm, but now take it a step further with this rule. Look for ways to be kind in all your small daily interactions. Remember from Chapter 6 that it is easy to get a little paranoid about what other people may think of you. Whatever they may or may not be thinking, little acts of kindness are the best ways to break down barriers.

Sometimes you need a bigger cure when the world is feeling too divisive. If you live in a big city like I do, you are likely surrounded by an unfortunate abundance of societal ills. In my city that would be homelessness. During the uptick in crossings at the southern border in 2018, I became acutely aware of the neglect suffered by my neighbors on the street, prompting me to volunteer at a homeless services center run by an Episcopal church near me. For a little more than a year I greeted clients, listened to their stories, and served meals. I helped some secure toiletries and pick out clean clothes. It is gratifying to do good, but there is something deeper here. There is a transformation of the heart that happens because you are treating each person as a human being with an individual history and the dignity of a soul. It goes beyond Rule #1 and embodies and extends our connection to others.

As a bonus for volunteering, you will meet people of all colors, some as fellow volunteers, some as persons you are helping.

RULE #5: THINK OF YOURSELF AS A BEARER OF LIGHT

This takes Rule #2 (Smile) and goes deeper. In Spanish, we say about a woman when announcing she has given birth, "*Ella dio la luz*" (literally, "she gave light"). Save us from those in America who want to start calling mothers "birthing persons!" Mothers are bearers of light.

I like to tell people on their birthdays, "You are the light of the world." It is a reminder that we carry the sacredness and specialness of life inside us, and we are meant to share it. I cannot help but think if raging protestors could understand the light inside them, we could make real progress on healing our divisions.

One way to remind yourself of your own light is to list all the ways you are something more than the color of your skin. I mean actually write down a list.

As an example, my list includes: Educator. Victor. World Traveler. Acquiring these identities required me to do something, to go out and become. You can do the same.

RULE #6: TRAVEL (AND DON'T TAKE PICTURES)

If classifying people by race or nationality is a disease, then travel is the cure. But not all travel is created equal, so a few tips could help.

Instagram is not a real place and therefore neither are the images posted there. When traveling, make a concerted effort to actually pay attention to the experience you are having. Also, travel alone if possible to a place completely foreign to you at least once in your lifetime. When you are in a group, you tend to stay isolated as a unit, and chances for meaningful interactions with the local people are missed.

Too many people travel as tourists, superficially skimming along the surface of another place and constantly using the camera as a barrier between themselves and the experience.

My journey through the Middle East after 9/11 was one of many meaningful travel experiences for me. I have had the great good fortune to have traveled the world to more than fifty countries across five continents. Experiencing other cultures unfiltered does more for breaking down barriers and eliminating stereotypes than anything else.

There is a difference between touring and traveling. The latter is becoming a lost art. To truly travel, put down your phone, grab a guidebook, struggle to speak with the locals when you don't know the language, and don't be afraid to go off the beaten path. My best experiences abroad happened when I did exactly that.

It brings to mind a bumpy ride in the back of a pickup truck in Aswan, Egypt. I had agreed to get my hands and feet dyed with henna by a Nubian girl. The whole experience culminated with an unexpected invitation to a traditional wedding deep in the heart of Nubian land. It was truly beautiful and unforgettable.

I also highly recommend using hostels for accommodations, the better to meet other humans and recognize them as individuals. The travel experiences I have cherished the most are swapping stories of discovery in the common lounge after a day of sightseeing or adventuring.

One of my quintessential hostel experiences was in Siwa Oasis, which is several hours west of Alexandria, in the Western Desert near the Libyan border. It is the home of the oracle of Ammon, made famous by Alexander the Great. I spent four days with a gaggle of strangers from a variety of countries, eating breakfast, lunch and dinner, swimming in salt pools, and exploring ancient ruins. It was one of my best experiences ever and one that reinforced that travel is the way to break down barriers between people.

RULE #7: TALK TO STRANGERS AND MAKE NEW FRIENDS

Maybe travel is not easy for you because of circumstances. Then "travel" where you are. Make an effort to talk to strangers. Bonus points if the person has a different viewpoint than you about race, politics, or education. (And, no, you don't need to discuss those topics.) Just find out what you have in common.

Some will turn into friends, and that might teach us all about the dangers of ideological blinders.

RULE #8: FORGIVE

Too many people walk around angry and despondent because of slights or wrongs that happened long ago. Some are even carrying around rage about things that happened generations before they were born.

I do not want to minimize this. Without a doubt, some people have been seriously victimized in their life. Certainly, history is filled with some real horrors. Some of those serious wrongs have unquestionably involved misguided and ill-informed ideas about race.

But how is what you are carrying around hurting you in the present? Can you imagine what it would be like to forgive? If that feels like it would be freeing, see if you can. There is nothing better for your soul—and your mental health—than being able to forgive in your heart.

One other thing to know about forgiveness: in some cases, it involves looking at our own role and responsibility. Sometimes we were wronged or slighted, but in a way that also involved our own disordered actions or thoughts. These situations can be the hardest to forgive because we also have to admit our own failures.

This may have particular relevance if you are trapped in a victim-oppressor mentality. Try a combination of forgiveness and honesty about yourself and see if it does not change your life.

RULE #9: DON'T CHECK BOXES

I mean this rule both literally and metaphorically. On the literal level, when completing forms, just ignore boxes asking about your race. Checking a box only serves to normalize constructed categories.

We accidentally reduce people to their race in other ways on an everyday basis, and we need to stop. For example, don't invoke skin color as a descriptor when it is not pertinent to the situation at hand (and it is almost always irrelevant). Many people are in the habit of saying things such as "a nice black woman at the store helped me find what I needed" or "my lawyer is a Hispanic guy" or "a white kid fixed my fence." What if we said instead, "a nice woman at the store helped me find what I needed" or "my lawyer is a nice guy" or "a kid fixed my fence"?

In most cases, race or skin color qualifiers are done almost unconsciously. But just like checking boxes, it reinforces the mistaken idea that our outward characteristics reflect the most important aspect of who we are.

RULE #10: DON'T LET ANYBODY TELL YOU WHO YOU ARE OR HOW TO IDENTIFY

In a world where bestselling books insist that you are either a racist or "antiracist"; in a world where the wrong tweet can get you fired; and in a world that insists today's America is a white supremacist nation, it can be hard to withstand the pressure to conform to racial orthodoxy.

Stand up against it anyway. You are not your race. Race is just a lie we keep telling ourselves. It is time to let go of the lie and turn to the truth of who we are: members of the human race.

FINAL THOUGHT

It is possible for us to end our preoccupation with race in America. It feels a long way off at the moment, but America has proven again and again to be a place of resilience and aspiration. We need enough people of goodwill to continue striving for that "more perfect Union."

Acknowledgments

I could not have done this book or anything else without the strength my faith gives me. May we all feel the grace and mercy as we work to heal our culture and country.

PRAYER FOR THE HUMAN RACE

O God our heavenly Father,
you have blessed us and given us dominion over all the earth:
Increase our reverence before the mystery of life;
and give us new insight into your purposes for the human race,
and new wisdom and determination in making provision
    for its future in accordance with your will;
through Jesus Christ our Lord.
Amen.

—BOOK OF COMMON PRAYER

About the Author

Born **FE LIZA RAMONE BENCOSME BENJAMIN** in New York City to Caribbean immigrants from the Cibao region of the Dominican Republic and St. Croix in the US Virgin Islands, Fe grew up moving among three cultures and around the world.

After a childhood blissfully unaware of skin color and racial conflict, Fe entered high school in the US. Through a series of negative experiences, she was forced to be aware of skin tones and "race" categories during her adolescence. Today, Fe is concerned by an ideology that foists a racialized worldview on children—robbing them of their sense of wonder and free lives, and jeopardizing the promise of a fully flourishing society.

Travel has afforded Fe a broad perspective of the world and its variety of peoples. She has traveled around the world several times, mostly on her own initiative, but also as part of her first career as a publicist for an international hotel corporation. Her travels also include a long sojourn in the Middle East following the events of 9/11 to learn more about the culture and its peoples during that time of conflict.

She began a second career as a teacher, and it was during her teacher preparation experience at George Mason University in Fairfax, Virginia, in the early 2010s that she encountered and was troubled by progressive theories in higher education. She would later encounter similar ideas at a doctoral program in Pennsylvania. Eventually, after a controversy over her race and identification with a teaching colleague, Fe left teaching altogether.

Today she lives in Houston, Texas, where she continues to encourage others to eschew racial identities by "not checking the box."

Lightning Source UK Ltd.
Milton Keynes UK
UKHW032117241022
411036UK00006B/73